LATI AMERICA

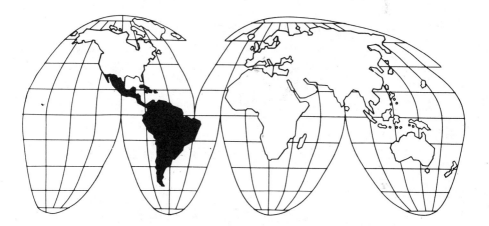

HISTORY, CULTURE, PEOPLE

LAWRENCE J. PAULINE
Social Studies Curriculum Consultant
Pearl River Public Schools, N.Y.

GLOBE BOOK COMPANY
A CAMBRIDGE TEXT
New York, Chicago, Cleveland

The revised edition of *Latin America: History, Culture, People* has been written by Daniel J. Mugan, Mr. Mugan is president of the Association of Teachers of Latin American Studies (ATLAS), and has travelled widely throughout Latin America. In 1972 and 1973 he directed the Fulbright-Hays Teacher Seminars in Mexico, and was Project Director of the Fulbright-Hays Seminar in Chile in 1980. He has also organized and directed programs for educators in Colombia and Cuba.

Series Consultant
HAROLD E. HAMMOND, Ph.D.

THE REGIONAL STUDIES SERIES
Africa
China
India-Pakistan-Bangladesh
Japan-Korea-Taiwan
Latin America
The Middle East
Southeast Asia
The Soviet Union

THIRD REVISED EDITION

ISBN: 0-87065-639-2

PRINTED IN THE UNITED STATES OF AMERICA
  4   5   6   7   8   9

INTRODUCTION

There is a tale told about instructions given by a wise old newspaper editor in London to a young foreign correspondent about to embark on his first assignment. The old editor finished his talk on quality reporting by saying, "Remember, if something happens to an Englishman, its a story. If something happens to ten Frenchmen, its a story. If something happens to one hundred Asians its a story, but nothing ever happens in Chile."

We now know, of course, that things do happen in Chile, and in Brazil, and in Cuba, and throughout Latin America. Not a day goes by when a story does not appear in the world press on the major events and changes in the region. Do we really understand the events shaping the future of Latin America? Do we realize that events in Latin America affect not only the people living there but the United States as well? The people and countries of Latin America have long suffered from the negative stereotype as the land of the *fiesta* and the *siesta*. The people of Latin America, as people everywhere in the world, are seeking a better life for themselves and their children. Our close geographic relationship together with a long history of past associations, and a common colonial heritage, tie our country with Latin America. As we approach the end of the twentieth century, an improved understanding of each other becomes more imperative than ever. In a world experiencing rapid change, and growing economic pressures, failure to do so could be a tragic mistake for both peoples.

This book is designed to contribute to a deeper understanding of Latin America by providing information and insights into the geography, history, and culture of the region. The impact of recent social, economic, and political trends in selected Latin American countries is also emphasized.

UNITED STATES

Rio Grande

○ Monterrey

Gulf of Mexico

ATLANTIC OCEAN

MEXICO

Guadalajara ○

Mexico City ★

Puebla ○

Havana

○ Nassau

★ **BAHAMAS**

CUBA

Kingston

Port-au-Prince

DOMINICAN REP.

Santo Domingo

San Juan

Puerto Rico

★ **ANTIGUA & BARBUDA**

BELIZE

Belmopan

HONDURAS

★ Tegucigalpa

Guatemala ○

GUATEMALA

Caribbean Sea

JAMAICA HAITI

San Salvador

EL SALVADOR

NICARAGUA

★ Managua

★ San Jose

COSTA RICA

PANAMA

Maracaibo

Panama

Roseau **DOMINICA**

★ Castries **ST. LUCIA**

ST. VINCENT Kingstown

GRENADA St. George's

★ Bridgetown **BARBADOS**

★ **TRINIDAD & TOBAGO**

Caracas ★

Port-of-Spain

VENEZUELA

GUYANA

Georgetown

SURINAME

Paramaribo

French Guiana

Cayenne

Bogotá ★

COLOMBIA

Galapagos Islands

Quito ★

Guayaquil ○

ECUADOR

Iquitos ○

Amazon R.

PACIFIC OCEAN

Lima ★

PERU

B R A Z I L

Recife ○

★ La Paz

BOLIVIA

Sucre

★ Brasília

Belo Horizonte ○

PARAGUAY

São Paulo ○

○ Rio de Janeiro

Asunción ★

ARGENTINA

Valparaíso ○

Santiago ★

Rosario ○

Buenos Aires ★

★ **URUGUAY**

Montevideo

CHILE

Rio de la Plata

N

W ✦ E

S

Miles

0   500   1000

0   804   1609

Kilometers

Latin America

🝖🝖 Falkland Islands

Cape Horn

CONTENTS

1

LATIN AMERICA: THE LAND

A. WHY IT IS CALLED "LATIN AMERICA"

The area south and southeast of the United States is called Latin America. Spanish is the official language in most of the countries of this region. In Brazil, the largest of all the Latin American countries, Portuguese is the official language. In Haiti, an island republic in the Caribbean, the people speak French. Because these languages stem from Latin, the language of ancient Rome, and because the Spanish and Portuguese cultures have influenced the regions, "Latin America" is the term generally used to name the area.

The term "Latin America" is not as precise as we would like it to be. When one considers that there are many sections throughout the region where the dominant culture is Indian or African, the word "Latin" does not seem to fit. In addition, English is the main language in a number of Caribbean countries, and Dutch is spoken in several places.

There are other Roman influences found in Latin America aside from languages. The civil code is based on Roman law and the French Code of Napoleon. Roman Catholicism is the official religion in most Latin American countries. Architecture shows Roman, Spanish, and Moorish influences. "Latin America" seems to be the only term broad enough to cover this diverse region.

There are 24 independent nations and several dependent countries in Latin America. The area can be divided into several parts. South America, for instance, includes all countries south of Panama; Central America is used to describe all countries north of South America and south of Mexico. Some of these are listed and defined on page 2:

1

Geographical Term	Area
Mexico	The land south of the United States border including Baja California
Central America	Guatemala, Belize, Honduras, El Salvador, Nicaragua, Costa Rica, Panama
West Indies	Bahama Islands, Greater Antilles, Lesser Antilles, Trinidad, Curaçao
Greater Antilles	Cuba, Haiti, Dominican Republic, Jamaica, Puerto Rico
Lesser Antilles	Virgin Islands, Leeward Islands, Windward Islands
South America	The 13 countries from the Panama border in the north to Cape Horn in the south
West Indies Associated States	Recent federation of most of the British islands in the Caribbean
Hispañola	The island including Haiti and the Dominican Republic
Bahama Islands	The 700 islands extending northwest and southeast from eastern Florida to a point north of Haiti
The Caribbean Countries	Those countries that touch the Caribbean Sea—from Venezuela in the south to Cuba in the north
The Andean Countries	Bolivia, Chile, Ecuador, Peru
The Countries of the Plata	Uruguay, Argentina
Pan-America	The United States and Latin America except for Cuba
Spanish America	The independent countries of Latin America where Spanish is the official language

B. TOPOGRAPHY

The Location of Latin America. If you had not located Latin America on a map you might have thought that it lies due south of the United States. Note the mistake you would have made. Looking closely at Latin America on the map or globe, you will see that nearly all of Latin America lies south and *east* of the United States. Thus, Latin America is located *southeast* of the United States. See where the meridian 75° west longitude cuts Latin America?

WESTERN HEMISPHERE

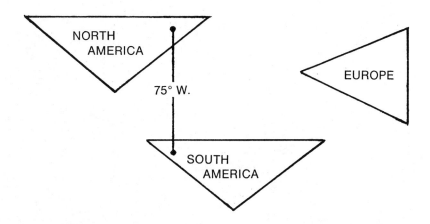

Another mistake is to think that Latin America is close to the United States. Although Mexico borders the United States, most of Latin America is far away. For example, Recife, Brazil, is the same distance from Miami, Florida, as it is from Moscow —4,800 miles. Another Brazilian city, Rio de Janeiro, is 4,792 miles from New Orleans, Louisiana. The northeast coast of Brazil is closer to Europe than to any part of the United States. Between New York and Buenos Aires, Argentina, it is 5,300 miles by air. From San Francisco to Santiago, Chile, it is 5,926 miles.

3

The Size of Latin America. Latin America is a vast area, stretching more than 6,000 miles from the northern tip of Mexico to Cape Horn at the southern tip of Argentina. Its greatest width—from eastern Brazil to northwestern Peru—is 3,100 miles. It covers nearly 800,000 square miles, an area slightly larger than that of the United States and Canada combined. Its countries range in size from Brazil, which is 200,000 square miles larger than the continental United States, to Haiti, which is the same size as Maryland.

LATIN AMERICA COMPARED IN SIZE WITH THE UNITED STATES

Latin America extends from latitude 33° North to latitude 56° South, and lies between the Atlantic and Pacific Oceans. A large part of Latin America lies between the Tropic of Cancer and the Tropic of Capricorn in the area which we call the tropical region or the *tropics*.

Its Mountains. A mountain chain, which we call the Rocky Mountains in the western part of the United States, extends southward through Mexico where it is called the Sierra Madres. In Mexico it separates into two chains between which is the central plateau. These mountains continue through Central America, dropping low at the Isthmus of Panama. In Colombia, where the chain is called the Andes Mountains, it rises abruptly again. The Andes, the "backbone" of the Latin American continent, are the longest closely joined mountain chain and the second highest range in the world. They are exceeded in height only by the Himalayas in Asia. Paralleling the Pacific Ocean, these mountains are largely volcanic. The mountains run along the entire 4,750 miles of the western coast of South America until they finally taper off into the Antarctic Ocean at Tierra del Fuego. The Andes vary in width from about 220 miles in Ecuador to about 400 miles in Bolivia.

The Andes have most of the highest mountain tops in the Western Hemisphere. The highest points reach 22,834 feet at Aconcagua, Argentina, 22,205 feet at Huascarán, Peru, and 22,162 feet at Bolivia's Mt. Tocorpuri. Although there are similar high peaks in Alaska, the highest peak in the continental United States is California's Mount Whitney, which is 14,495 feet high. The Andes have 50 peaks over 20,000 feet high. They stretch like a three-to-four-mile-high wall from north to south. Travel in the mountains in an east to west direction is almost impossible. The existing mountain passes are either narrow and two to three miles above sea level, often blocked by snow several months of the year, or they are largely uninhabited, dense rain forests. In Peru and Bolivia it is not uncommon to see snow-capped mountain tops. A railroad and the Pan-American

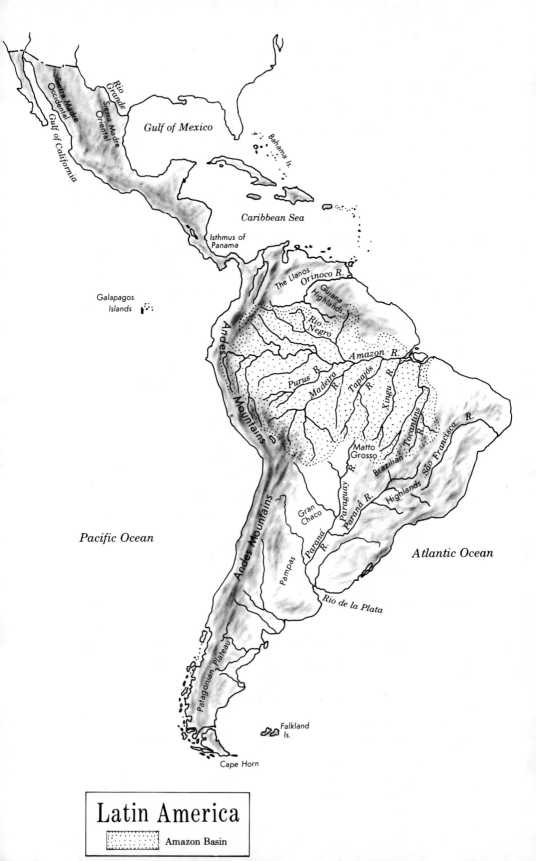

Gulf of Mexico

Sierra Madre Occidental

Sierra Madre Oriental

Rio Grande

Gulf of California

Bahama Is.

Caribbean Sea

Isthmus of Panama

Galapagos Islands

The Llanos

Orinoco R.

Guiana Highlands

Rio Negro

Amazon R.

Andes Mountains

Purus R.

Madeira R.

Tapajós R.

Xingu R.

Tocantins R.

São Francisco R.

Brazilian Highlands

Matto Grosso

Pacific Ocean

Gran Chaco

Paraguay R.

Paraná R.

Atlantic Ocean

Pampas

Paraná R.

Rio de la Plata

Patagonian Plateau

Falkland Is.

Cape Horn

Latin America

.... Amazon Basin

Highway run through the largest pass, Uspallata Pass, to connect Santiago, Chile, and Buenos Aires, Argentina. Other passes include less direct railroads and trail-like roads. River transportation is the preferred method of travel.

The Rivers and Lakes. Besides the Andes Mountain chain, the other chief geographical feature of Latin America is the Amazon River and its tributaries. The Amazon River, the world's second longest river (surpassed only by the Nile in Africa), flows for 3,900 miles; most of its length is in Brazil. It has more than 200 branches and tributaries which reach into Venezuela, Colombia, Ecuador, Peru, and Bolivia. Beginning in the Peruvian Andes, only 100 miles east of the Pacific Ocean, the Amazon generally follows the line of the equator from west to east, although it occasionally flows from north to south. It empties into the Atlantic Ocean 2,000 miles away, where its mouth is 207 miles wide. In the mouth or delta of the Amazon is Marajó Island, which is as large as the states of New Hampshire and Vermont combined.

The discharge of fresh water at the mouth of the Amazon is about 12 times that of the Mississippi River. The Amazon drains 20 percent of the total fresh water in the world.

The Amazon's main tributaries are immense rivers in their own right. The largest northward-flowing tributaries are the Xingu, 1,800 miles long; Tapajóz, 1,800 miles long; Madeira, 2,100 miles long; Purús, 2,000 miles long; and Juruá, 1,500 miles long. The main southward-flowing tributaries are the Japurá, 1,500 miles, and Rio Negro, 1,400 miles. These tributaries pour millions of tons of water into the Amazon River.

Although the Amazon River and its tributaries are huge and have vast potential for resource development, year-round rain, tropical heat, and the jungle have made the river banks almost uninhabitable. As a result, in spite of the fact that ocean steamers can sail a thousand miles up the broad channel of the Ama-

7

zon, the surrounding area is inhabited mostly by primitive tribes of Indians.

A second important river is Rio de la Plata—the "River of Silver"—which is formed by the Paraná and Uruguay rivers. Actually, it is more an estuary than a river. Estuaries are arms or outlets of the sea and make excellent harbors. Ocean tides extend up into the river mouth and carry away the river's silt. The Rio de la Plata drains an area of 1,500,000 square miles in parts of Argentina, Bolivia, Brazil, Uruguay and all of Paraguay. It is second only to the Amazon in the volume of water it empties into the Atlantic Ocean. The most important ports on the Rio de la Plata are Buenos Aires and Montevideo. Buenos Aires, the capital of Argentina, lies on its southwestern shore and Montevideo, the capital of Uruguay, is on its northern shore. From these ports most of the meat and grain from Argentina and Uruguay are shipped abroad. Although the river varies in depth from only 8 to 18 feet, it is navigable for more than 3,000 miles.

The Orinoco is the third largest river system in South America. Rising in the Andes Mountains, it snakes for about 1,500 miles through southern Venezuela and empties into the Atlantic Ocean off the northern coast of Venezuela. The Orinoco drains some 450,000 square miles—most of Venezuela and one-fourth of Colombia. Ciudad Bolivar is the most important city on the Orinoco Basin, even though it is 270 miles upstream from the river's swampy mouth. The Orinoco rushes into the Atlantic with such force that soil and silt may be seen in the ocean 20 miles offshore.

There are few large lakes in Latin America. Lake Maracaibo in northwest Venezuela is in a petroleum-producing area. Lake Titicaca, the largest, is located on a high plateau 12,644 feet above sea level, bordering Peru and Bolivia. It is large enough for ships to travel on it.

The Importance of Geographic Factors. Geographic factors have a decided effect upon the people and the way of life in

CASE INQUIRY: The Role of Geography

For many years geographers have discussed the question of geographic determinism: does geography *determine* the way people live? (*make* life follow certain patterns); or does it merely *influence* life style by limiting possibilities? See what the author of the following selection seems to feel.

The eastern mountains, old and worn by wind and rain, include the highlands which reach from the northern coastal states of Ceará and Pernambuco through Bahia and Minas Gerais to the southern state of Rio Grande do Sul. Here are no such lofty peaks as adorn the western cordillera: the highest are only some 9,400 feet. The Brazilian highlands crowd close to the coast at Santos, Rio de Janeiro, and Bahia, erecting a jagged coastal wall, the Serra do Mar, which long served to confine the population to this scallop fringe . . .

The mountains and their high plateaus have largely determined the political, economic, and social patterns of much of Latin America. The Andes' high barriers established the boundaries of Chile and Argentina. The plateaus and inaccessible valleys furnished refuge to aboriginal [original or native] peoples, delayed their conquest by European invaders, and helped to preserve their ancient ways. Furthermore, the existence of great expanses of high plateaus and valleys has gone far toward offsetting Latin America's chief climatic liability—the fact that three-quarters of its total area lies between the Tropics of Cancer and Capricorn. In Mexico, Central America, and the Andean republics the majority of the people live on the cool tablelands from four to twelve thousand feet above the steaming tropics at sea level. In Brazil, too, the vigor of the people of São Paulo and Minas Gerais—almost one-third of all Brazilians—may be largely credited to the temperate climate of those highlands.

1. What benefits does Dr. Herring say are derived from the highlands of Latin America? What hardships do you think mountains and plateaus create?

2. Do you think such geographical areas *influence* or *determine* a people's way of life? Discuss in terms of life in areas you know.

A History of Latin America by Hubert Herring. Alfred A. Knopf, New York, 1961, pages 6-8.

Latin America. Although there is a vast network of roads known as the Pan-American Highway system, and a few railroads extend throughout Mexico, Central America, and South America, transportation and communication have been hindered largely by the great Andes Mountain chain. The high plateaus, mountain peaks, and tropical rain forests have made development very difficult. Generally speaking, the people are poor and must usually transport goods to market on their own backs. Throughout Latin America, women may be seen carrying wares on their heads. Occasionally, burros are used as beasts of burden.

The vast mountains, long unnavigable rivers, tropical forests and lack of roads isolate Latin Americans from each other as well as from the rest of the world.

C. THE REGIONS

Patagonian Plateau. The Patagonian Plateau, located in the southern part of South America between the Colorado River in Argentina and Tierra del Fuego, includes a small portion of Chile and the southern quarter of Argentina. Patagonia takes its name from the large feet *(patagones)* of the Indians of the plateau. The area has deep canyons and a rocky, rugged terrain rising to an altitude of 5,000 feet near the base of the Andes Mountains. Transportation throughout Patagonia is by means of its airlines and good railway service.

The Pampas. Directly north of Patagonia lie the pampas, a huge 250,000-square-mile grass-covered, treeless plain that stretches across Argentina from the Atlantic coast to the Andes. The pampas are similar to the steppes of Eurasia and the prairies of North America. On the map, the pampas are located from 30° to 40° south latitude. They appear to be flat because they slope very gradually over a 635-mile distance from 2,000 feet in the west to 20 feet above sea level in the east. This area is divided into two zones—the western dry pampas, which are almost barren and semi-desert, and the eastern humid pampas, the most prosperous and important agricultural region in Argentina. In its rich, fertile soil, corn and wheat are grown, and its coarse-leaf grass is ideal food for sheep and cattle.

The Gran Chaco. Blending into the pampas on the north is the Gran Chaco, which includes parts of northern Argentina, southern Bolivia, southwestern Brazil and most of Paraguay. If you were to fly over this vast 200,000-square-mile area, you would see mostly flat land. There are some grassy plains and jungles which are still inhabited by a few Indian tribes, mainly the Guaraní. Most of the region is undeveloped and of little economic value because of its extreme climate, its remote location, and the prevalence of disease. However, easy and inexpensive water transportation has made possible the development of the regions in Paraguay and Argentina along the Paraguay-Paraná River. The forests provide tannin and timber. Several crops, particularly Paraguayan tea called *yerba maté,* and Argentinian cotton, are grown in this region.

Ownership of this large area was disputed for years; border clashes among the countries included in the Gran Chaco were frequent. The last major conflict, between Paraguay and Bolivia, ended in 1935. By a treaty of 1938, Paraguay was ceded 92,000 square miles of Bolivian territory.

The Brazilian Highlands. East of the Gran Chaco and south of the Amazon lie the vast plateau uplands known as the Brazilian Highlands. Most of the country's richest farmland, its mineral reserves, and its population centers are located along the eastern margins of the highlands. São Paulo, Rio de Janeiro, Santos, Porto Alegre, Salvador, and Recife are the great cities of Brazil. The plains of this tableland are not as high as the plateaus in the Andes; they rise only 1,000 to 9,500 feet above sea level. The Brazilian Highlands border the South Atlantic Ocean for nearly 2,000 miles along the coast and stretch far into the interior.

The Mato Grosso. The *Mato Grosso* ("great woods") stretch across southwestern Brazil and border on the countries of Bolivia and Paraguay. Most of the *Mato Grosso* lies on the Brazilian plateau in an area of 484,486 square miles. There are tropical rain forests in the north and a swampy floodplain in the south. It is well-known for its excellent grazing lands; agriculture and livestock represent its chief economic assets. The major cities of the *Mato Grosso* plateau are Cuiabá, Corumbá, and Campo Grande. Its navigable rivers include the São Lourenco, Cuiabá, Paraná and Paraguay.

The Amazon Basin. Almost all of northern Brazil is occupied by the drainage basin of the Amazon River and its major branches. It is the largest soil and silt lowland area in the world and covers 2,722,000 square miles in six countries. To the north are the Guiana Highlands; in the south are the Brazilian Highlands; and in the west are the Andes.

The most impressive surface feature in Brazil is the immense equatorial or tropical rain forest which covers almost the entire country. There the temperature is high every month of the year. The rain forest lies on and near the equator, and the air is intensely heated because at the equator the sun is always directly overhead. It rains almost every day of the year, and the nights are long, hot, and humid. There is no change of seasons. The daily heat and rain cause plants to grow very rapidly. It is not unusual to see trees 100 feet tall with climbing and trailing vines beneath them. Because the trees are so high, little sunlight reaches the forest floor making it impossible for smaller plants to grow. With few smaller plants to hold the rainwater, it seeps into the ground, dissolves salts and minerals in the soil and brings them to the surface. This process is called "leaching." The leached soil kills off smaller vegetation and gives trees the opportunity to grow to such tremendous heights. Wherever sunlight falls on a clearing, weeds grow so quickly that they crowd out crops; thus farming is impossible.

The area abounds in monkeys, brilliantly colored parrots, strange animals like the tapir and sloth, and many insects.

Here and there, primitive Indian tribes have made clearings for tapping rubber or collecting tague nuts. Sometimes the Indians burn the trees and plant manioc and bananas in the burned area. The heavy rains wash the soil away. Then the Indian tribes move to new clearings, and the jungle fills in the old ones.

However, the rain forest does yield valuable wood—ebony, mahogany, rosewood, and Spanish cedar—used in the manufacture of furniture. The crude rubber obtained from the sap of at least two varieties of trees is another important product of the forest. One product—carnauba wax—from which phonograph records and electric insulation are made, is exported to the United States in great quantity.

Some habitable areas have been carved out of the Basin. The chief concentration of people is in the cities of Manaus and Belém, but the average population density of the region is only about two people per square mile. Washington, D.C., in comparison, has about 12,000 people to the square mile. Brasília, one of the most modern cities in the world has been carved out of the great rain forest in central Brazil. This new capital of Brazil has all the modern conveniences and is connected to the coast by a new highway.

The Llanos. This Spanish-American term refers to the tropical savanna or grassland regions north of the Amazon equatorial rain forests in Venezuela and eastern Colombia. These grass-covered plains extend 600 miles east to west from the Atlantic Ocean to the Andes, and 200 miles from the coastal ranges of the north to the Orinoco River in the south, covering an area of 100,000 square miles.

The *Llanos* have a wet and dry season. During the rainy season much of the area is under 12 to 15 feet of water because the rivers overflow their banks; it is necessary to build villages on high ground. During the dry season the grass turns brown and the soil is parched. Although valuable orchids grow here, the typical vegetation of the area is a coarse, rough grass which is ideal for large herds of cattle, the region's main export.

A Latin American "cowboy," called a *llanero,* rounds up cattle on the flat, treeless llanos.

The people who live on these plains are called *llaneros,* descendants of Spanish colonists and Indians. They are skilled horsemen and hardy, tough cattlemen. Recently, many other Latin Americans have migrated to this potentially rich region— rich in grazing land and untapped minerals.

D. CLIMATE AND RAINFALL

Most of Latin America enjoys a tropical or warm climate because three-quarters of the land area fall within the Tropics of Cancer and Capricorn. It is, therefore, largely within the range of the equatorial rain forests and the trade winds. In fact, all of the countries except Chile have jungles.

In addition to having a tropical climate, Latin America has a *vertical* climate. That is, the temperature drops approximately 3° F. for every 1,000 feet rise in altitude up to 30,000 feet. Therefore, the three great highland regions of Latin America are livable even though they are on the equator. The snow-capped Andes have all varieties of climate, from a tropical climate at their base to a temperate climate on the slopes and perpetual snow on the peaks. Thus, the altitude of land forms directly affects temperature and rainfall.

Other factors which affect Latin America's climate are its

mountain barriers, ocean currents, and high and low pressure areas.

In the Latin American countries south of the equator, which includes most of South America, the seasons are the reverse of ours. Their winter is our summer and vice versa.

Climate in the West Indies. The West Indies are a tropical area; east winds constantly bring warm air over the islands. The temperature varies from season to season ranging from 71° to 85° F. In the cool month of January the temperature rarely falls below 71° F.; in warm July the temperature rarely climbs

CLIMATES OF LATIN AMERICA

above 85° F. The trade winds blowing in from the sea keep the temperature relatively cool. In the more mountainous islands of the West Indies the climate is cooler, making them summer resort areas.

While temperature does not vary greatly among the islands, rainfall does vary. The average annual rainfall is from 40 to 250 inches. The higher islands tend to receive the most rainfall and the low-lying islands receive the least. The moisture-laden winds cool as they rise and cause heavy rainfall on the windward (eastern) slopes. The protected leeward (western) slopes are relatively dry. In Jamaica, for example, the windward slopes receive 244 inches of rain per year while the leeward slopes receive only 29 inches. It is not surprising, then, that most of the people live on the leeward side of the islands.

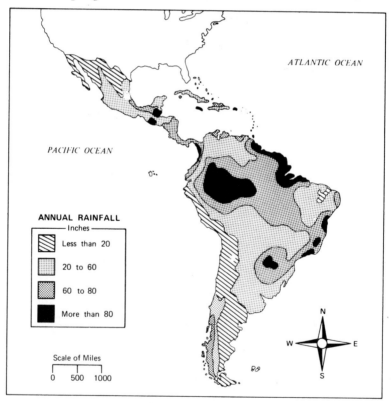

ANNUAL RAINFALL OF LATIN AMERICA

From June to October of each year the people of the West Indies watch for hurricanes. These tropical storms contain enormous amounts of rain and their winds travel at more than 75 miles per hour. They rise in the south Atlantic and the Gulf of Mexico and blow toward the West Indies. Then they turn toward North America.

Ships and weather stations report where hurricanes are forming; they are tracked by radar-equipped airplanes which fly in the areas where hurricanes are known to breed. More recently weather satellites have helped to warn of approaching hurricanes. In 1979, Hurricane "David" hit the Dominican Republic, killing more than 600 people and leaving another 225,000 homeless.

The Climate in Mexico. Mexico has three vertical climate zones named *tierra caliente, tierra templada,* and *tierra fria. Tierra caliente,* which means "hot land," includes the coastal regions and extends from sea level to 3,000 feet above sea level. In this hot, tropical region the temperature seldom falls below 70° F. and may soar above 100° F. Above this zone is the *tierra templada* which means "temperate lands." This area extends to about 6,000 feet and has a mild climate. The average annual temperature ranges from 60° to 77° F. Mexico City, the center of government and population, is located on this central Mexican plateau. The rainfall of this area is light and the climate is cool because of its elevation.

The area where it is cold all year round extends from 6,000 feet to the snow line, above which there is usually snow, and includes the higher parts of the Mexican plateau. This zone is called *tierra fria,* meaning "cold land," and has an average annual temperature of 15° F., although the climate varies more in this region than in the other two. At the same elevation frosts may occur while sub-tropical vegetation grows several miles away. At this higher elevation there is a rainy and a dry season. Most of the rain falls in the *tierra caliente* during the wet season, called *invierno,* although it is actually summer. The dry season, which includes the winter, is called *verano.*

Tropical trade winds blow across a large part of Mexico. These winds pick up moisture as they cross the Gulf of Mexico and head toward the mainland. The eastern mountain slopes and coastal plains receive heavy downpours. The winds lose most of their moisture by the time they reach the plateau, making this area semi-arid.

The varying physical features of Mexico account for the diversity of climate. Tropical grasslands and an equatorial rain forest are found on the Isthmus of Tehuantepec, parts of Yucatán, and nearby coastal areas. Desert areas are found in Baja California and northern Mexico between the Rio Grande and Monterrey.

The Climate in Central America. Central America, which includes the countries of Belize, Costa Rica, El Salvador, Guatemala, Honduras, Nicaragua, and Panama, has a vertical climate similar to that of Mexico. Central America is divided into three zones: *tierra caliente, tierra templada,* and *tierra fria.*

Tierra caliente includes the eastern lowlands bordering the Caribbean Sea. The lowlands are hot and always wet. The gusty winds of the Atlantic bring their moisture to this area, and it is not uncommon for the region to receive over 100 inches of rain per year. Temperatures average 75° F. The Pacific lowlands have a drier climate because of their location on the leeward side of the mountains. The rainfall is seasonal, averaging about 70 inches per year. Much of the land is used for pasture.

The Central American highlands, or the *tierra templada* zone, have a mild seasonal climate. This is where most of the people live. The great coffee plantations are in this area. In the *tierra fria* the temperature averages between 55° and 65° F.

The Climate of South America. South America has a pattern of many different types of climate—steaming tropical jungles, rolling grasslands, hot and humid coasts, cool tablelands, dry deserts, and snow-covered mountains. Within almost every country dramatic contrasts can be found. Long, narrow Chile is a desert in the north, has a climate like that of California in the

18

For commercial purposes, some trees of this Amazonian forest were destroyed to stimulate growth of more valuable trees.

United Nations

central part, and is much like the wooded part of the eastern United States in the south. South America can be divided into five regions for climate study.

1. *Amazon Basin.* The temperature averages about 80° F. Rainfall varies from 70-80 inches in the lower Amazon Basin to 100 inches in the Guiana Highlands.

2. *The Coastlands.* The Caribbean and Atlantic coasts are hot and rainy in all seasons. The rainfall averages 40 inches a year.

3. *The Highlands.* The Andean mountain ranges have a vertical climate. The Brazilian and Guiana tablelands are lower but high enough to be cool. This area is ideal for growing coffee.

4. *The Pampas.* These grassy slopes have a wide variety of climate—from extreme humidity to cool, dry weather. They receive rain from the trade winds. Much of the area is in the temperate zone.

5. *The Wastelands.* South America has many miles of desert wastes. The trade winds are drained dry of rain

by the Andes Mountains and so bring no moisture inland. The greatest wasteland, the Atacama Desert in Chile, is rich in copper and sodium nitrate, but its burning sands will support little life. An occasional oasis can be found in places where short, swift rivers flow from the Andes into the Pacific Ocean. These islands of green among the burning sands are planted with cotton, sugar, and tropical fruits.

Also dry are the western part of Argentina and the southern part, Patagonia. The southwestern part of South America is in the path of the westerly winds, and so its Pacific coast has plenty of rain and is thickly forested.

Severe winters, as we know them in the United States, are absent from South America. This is because of the influence of the ocean and the fact that most of South America is in the low latitudes.

E. AGRICULTURE—THE WAY OF LIFE

Agriculture is the way of life for most of the people in Latin America. Farming is quite varied. Practically every well-known crop is grown there—corn, bananas, coffee, sugarcane, and vegetables. Horses, cattle, sheep, llamas, and alpacas are raised. The export of agricultural products and their by-products is one of Latin America's chief economic resources.

Farming in the West Indies. Agriculture—both subsistence farming and plantation agriculture—is the main occupation of the West Indians. Subsistence farming for personal and family use is done on small patches on steep hillsides. The larger land areas are used for plantation agriculture where products are grown for export, generally financed by foreign capital. Sugarcane and its by-products, rum and alcohol, are the chief crops of the West Indies.

Thousands of workers on the large sugar plantations harvest

the sugarcane with sharp *machetes* (knives). It is then taken to the refinery where the raw sugar is extracted, washed, dried, and packed. While most of the West Indian countries produce sugar and its by-products, other crops are grown for export. These crops include tobacco from Cuba and the Dominican Republic, coffee from Haiti, and bananas from Jamaica.

Farming in Central America. Most of the people of Central America are subsistence farmers who grow just enough food for their families. Bananas are one of the chief export crops; most of them are sent north to the United States. Bananas grow best in hot, humid areas and are, therefore, grown on coastal plantations in the tropical lowlands of Central America.

Banana plants are 10 to 20 feet tall. After a year of growth they produce flowers on a stem. It is from these flowers that

A· Livestock Ranching
B· Shifting and Rudimental Sedentary Cultivation
C· Commercial Plantation Cropping
D· Subsistence Livestock and Crop Farming
E· Non-Agricultural Areas
F· Fishing

Scale of Miles
0   500   1000

ATLANTIC OCEAN

PACIFIC OCEAN

N
W   E
S

AGRICULTURE MAP OF LATIN AMERICA

21

bananas grow. The stem becomes very heavy and bends toward the ground as the bananas grow larger. The whole stem is cut off from the plant while the bananas are unripe and green. They are transported by railroad to the coast and shipped by boat to the United States. Banana boats are refrigerated to keep the fruit from ripening too quickly. Upon arrival in the United States, the bananas are immediately sent to food stores before they become ripe enough to eat.

Cacao, from which chocolate is made, is grown mainly for export in Costa Rica. The cacao beans grow in pods on the trunk of the cacao tree. The pods are gathered and cut open and the beans are extracted, dried, roasted and ground. Milk and sugar are then added to make chocolate. Coffee is another cash crop grown in the highlands of Central America for export to the United States. Other crops are beans, cotton, rice, and sugarcane.

Farming in South America.   Only about a quarter of the land in South America is suitable for farming, yet more than half of the people make their living from it. Three distinct farming zones are found at different altitudes. In the high altitudes over 5,000 feet above sea level, grains such as wheat, maize, rye, and barley are grown. Coffee is grown on the cool plateaus below 5,000 feet. In the tropical and subtropical hot and humid areas near sea level are grown the great plantation crops— bananas, cacao, rice, sugar, and cotton.

Although sheep, llamas, and alpacas graze in the Andes, agriculture is not carried on extensively there because of the cold weather. However, extensive farming does take place in valleys and on plateaus where cattle and horses are raised and grain is grown. On the lower slopes cotton, sugarcane, and coffee are raised. Fruits and vegetables are grown on terraces. These are earthen steps cut into the mountainsides to keep water from flowing off. Water for crops and animals comes from cool mountain steams by means of irrigation ditches. They trap the water and direct it to the fields.

The highlands of Patagonia are used mainly for sheep-grazing

Plantation agriculture is the mainstay of many countries in Latin America. In Costa Rica, sugarcane is brought to the mill (top, left); a warehouse in Columbia prepares coffee for export (top, right); and workers harvest bananas on a plantation in Nicaragua (bottom).

because their cool, dry climate produces excellent grazing lands. A large irrigation system has made the raising of grain, sugar cane, and coffee possible.

F.   THE CRISIS IN AGRICULTURE

In terms of major exports of agriculture, the statistics of Latin America are impressive. Latin America grows nearly 75 percent of the world's coffee, over 60 percent of the world's banana crop, and 25 percent of the world's sugar supply.

Despite these figures and the fact that almost one half of the area's working population is engaged in agriculture, the countries of Latin America are not yet able to provide enough food for their rapidly growing populations. During the 1970's, Colombia reported that except for wheat production, food yields declined. During the same period Venezuela was importing half of its meat, corn, and milk supply. Bolivia found it necessary to import one half of all its food stuffs.

The causes of the crisis in agriculture in Latin America are related to the history of the region, inefficient farming techniques, and the lack of modern technology. Perhaps the most important of these is the legacy of the past—the system of landholding, which is known by names as *estancias, haciendas,* and *fundos,* but is best known as the *latifundia.*

The Root Causes.   During the period of the Spanish Conquest, *encomiendas,* or grants of land, were awarded to the *conquistadores* for services to the Crown. *Encomiendas* were originally intended as an award for a specific number of years. By the eighteenth century, however, *encomiendas* were recognized as properties that could be inherited. The Church became the primary landholder in this system of land grants as it received grants from the Crown and inherited estates of the deceased faithful.

Following independence, however, much of the Church's landholdings were transferred to individual landlords who, more often than not, became absentee owners. The absentee owners tended to have an indifferent attitude toward the *latifundios.*

Because they benefited from the very low paid peasant labor, the absentee owners were not anxious to invest in machinery for higher crop yields.

The tenants on the other hand, saw no need to do more than engage in subsistence farming. They produced enough to meet the costs of their basic needs. Farmers other than tenant farmers usually were able to afford no more than tiny pieces of land that have come to be known as *minifundios*. In this system, farming was done on a very inefficient and subsistence level. This problem continues to hinder agriculture development in Latin America today.

Agriculture Reform. Over the past fifty years one of the most controversial issues in Latin America has been the crisis in agriculture. The name given to the solution is "Agricultural Reform." In 1917, Mexico was the first Latin American nation to attempt a solution. Large tracts of land were broken up and redistributed to Mexico's peasants as *ejidos*. The results of the land reform program in Mexico have been mixed and the controversy continues.

Supporters of reform argue that land redistribution will improve crop yields, make the society more stable (by having large numbers of people engaged in economic self-interest), and finally, reduce the likelihood of revolution. Those who oppose land reform say breaking up large estates is inefficient and will lead to the merger of small farms and the creation of large growing areas. Today, most of the Latin American nations have some kind of land reform programs. But making the reform programs work requires more vigorous enforcement.

G. MINERAL RESOURCES

More than 90 percent of Latin America's export earnings come from the sale of foodstuffs and minerals. Latin America is a region rich in mineral resources. Brazil has the world's largest reserves of manganese, Chile is the second largest copper producing nation in the world, and Mexico is said to have a

MINERAL RESOURCES

Country	Resources
Argentina	coal, lead, zinc, iron, silver, copper, gold, petroleum
Bolivia	tin, silver, copper, lead, tungsten, zinc, petroleum, antimony
Brazil	quartz, beryl, mica, manganese, iron, gold, oil, nickel, diamonds
Belize	none
Caribbean Islands	asphalt, petroleum
Chile	nitrates, copper, iron, oil, gold, silver
Colombia	petroleum, emeralds, platinum, gold, silver, copper, lead
Costa Rica	gold, silver, quartz, alabaster, granite, oil
Cuba	iron, copper, manganese, chromium, nickel
Ecuador	silver, petroleum, copper, iron, lead, coal
El Salvador	gold, silver, copper, lead, zinc
French Guiana	gold, bauxite
Guatemala	silver, gold, copper, iron, lead, zinc
Guyana	bauxite, gold, iron, diamonds, manganese, mica
Haiti	bauxite, copper, gold, silver
Honduras	gold, silver, copper, lead, zinc, iron
Mexico	silver, gold, copper, lead, zinc, antimony, petroleum, manganese, mercury, vanadium
Nicaragua	gold, oil
Panama	manganese, gold, silver, lead, aluminum, copper
Paraguay	iron, manganese, copper
Peru	copper, steel, petroleum, antimony, gold, lead, vanadium, zinc
Surinam	oil, bauxite, aluminum
Uruguay	gold, copper, lead, manganese
Venezuela	pearls, oil, iron, gold, copper, coal, salt, asphalt

petroleum reserve greater than any to be found in the Middle East. Large reserves of high grade iron ore in Venezuela are still waiting to be mined. Latin America lacks high grade coal deposits so vital to the development of industry. This factor and the lack of adequate transportation systems needed to move the extracts from the mines to the facories are obstacles to development.

QUESTIONS AND ACTIVITIES

KEY WORDS AND PHRASES

Can you explain the meaning of the following words or phrases? Use a dictionary if necessary.

tributary	silt	tropics	vertical climate
drainage basin	plateau	leaching	*tierra fria*
delta	steppes	savanna	"slash and burn"
tropical rain forest	highlands	*llaneros*	*hacienda*
agricultural reform	Iberian		

MULTIPLE CHOICE TEST

In each of the following you have four possible answer choices. Select the only correct answer.

1. Which of the following is an explanation for the name "Latin" America? *(a)* The main language of the area is Latin. *(b)* The languages of the first white settlers came from Latin. *(c)* Students must take Latin in high school. *(d)* The Roman Catholic Church has a mass in Latin.
2. All the following are considered a part of the Greater Antilles *except* *(a)* Cuba, *(b)* Haiti, *(c)* Puerto Rico, *(d)* Virgin Islands.
3. Which of the following are Andean countries? *(a)* Bolivia and Argentina, *(b)* Chile and Peru, *(c)* Ecuador and Brazil, *(d)* Guyana and Venezuela.
4. Most South Americans live near the *(a)* coast, *(b)* interior, *(c)* rivers, *(d)* mountains.

5. Most of the Amazon River flows through (a) Venezuela, (b) Colombia, (c) Brazil, (d) Bolivia.
6. The two other major rivers of South America are the Orinoco and the (a) Juruá, (b) La Plata, (c) Purús, (d) Madeira.
7. The mountains and rivers have greatly affected Latin American development because they (a) are used as travel routes to the interior, (b) provide ideal weather conditions, (c) provide excellent means of communication, (d) serve as barriers to transportation and commerce.
8. The geography of Latin America gives its people a feeling of (a) internationalism, (b) communism, (c) socialism, (d) isolation.
9. The tropical storms with winds more than 75 mph are called (a) hurricanes, (b) tornadoes, (c) cyclones, (d) twisters.
10. The greatest influence on weather in the West Indies is the (a) sun, (b) snow-capped mountains, (c) wind, (d) ocean.

MATCHING QUESTIONS

In the space at the left, write the letter of the phrase in Column B that best matches each item in Column A.

Column A	Column B
.... 1. Patagonian Plateau	a. Bolivia and Paraguay fought over this
.... 2. pampas	b. Excellent grazing lands and the city of Cuibá
.... 3. Gran Chaco	c. Primarily a sheep-raising region located between the Andes Mountains and the Atlantic Ocean
.... 4. Brazilian Highlands	
.... 5. Mato Grosso	d. Tropical savanna or grasslands north of the Amazon rain forest
.... 6. Amazon Basin	e. Grassy plain in Argentina ideal for raising cattle
.... 7. Llanos	f. Rio de Janeiro is located in this rich farmland
	g. Tropical rain forest on or near the equator

28

TRUE OR FALSE

Do you agree or disagree with the following statements? Give reasons for your answers.

.... 1. In the *tierra caliente* temperature seldom falls below 70°F.
.... 2. Tropical trade winds blow across a large part of Mexico.
.... 3. Western mountain slopes receive a heavy rainfall in Central America.
.... 4. A vertical climate is present in the plateau of Mexico.
.... 5. Most of Baja California is cool with plenty of rainfall.
.... 6. The eastern lowlands bordering the Caribbean are cool and dry.
.... 7. The Pacific lowlands have a dry climate.
.... 8. Most people live on the windward side of mountains.
.... 9. Severe winters do not occur in South America.
........10. The climate of South America is always hot and dry.

THINGS TO DO

1. Prepare a map of Latin America. Locate and label all countries, important rivers, and mountains.
2. Research Project: Why have most civilizations started along river systems?
3. Visit the local travel agency and obtain brochures concerning the West Indies. Prepare a bulletin board display of these materials.
4. Present a report on hurricanes and the damage they have done. Draw a diagram of a hurricane.
5. Prepare an oral report on how bananas are grown and marketed, and how chocolate is produced.
6. Imagine that you are a worker with a family on a *hacienda*. Describe a typical day in your life. This may require research in other books in your school library.
7. Prepare a report on how natural disasters have affected Latin America; include droughts, earthquakes, and floods.
8. In committee, prepare a series of clear plastic overlays to compare the size of Latin America with that of the United States.
9. Prepare a graph which shows the vertical climate of Latin America and the agricultural products and livestock that result.

PRE-COLUMBIAN INDIAN CIVILIZATIONS

2

When Christopher Columbus and his crew sailed their ships into the waters of the New World, they helped create a confusion over language that still exists today. Columbus had been searching for a new route to Asia and upon sighting the islands of the Caribbean believed he had reached the "Indies." He gave the name "Indians" to the people he met upon landing. Today, we still call those islands in the Caribbean the "West Indies." The word "Indian" is also fixed in our vocabulary as a term identifying the native American.

There is difficulty with the word "Indian," however. It has become a broad term applied to all of the peoples living in the New World before the Spanish. It thus fails to make distinctions among the varied cultures and civilizations that existed there. Try to imagine someone using the word "European" to refer to the variety of peoples that live on that continent. Is there no difference between a Swede and a person living in Greece? Perhaps now you can understand why the word "Indian" is not an accurate word to describe the native peoples of the Americas.

As the Spanish began their conquest of the New World, they met a number of cultural groups such as the Carib of the Caribbean area, the Chibcha of Colombia, the Auraucanian of Chile, and the Guarani of Paraguay. Perhaps the best known of all these groups were the Mayas, the Aztecs, and the Inca.

A. THE MAYAS, AZTECS AND INCAS

The Mayas. Historians studying the Mayas usually analyze two distinct times in their past. During the Classic Period, from

The culture of the Mayan civilization in Mexico and Central America can be seen in the Temple of Inscriptions (top, left); a stone engraving of a Mayan villager (top, right); a huge Olmec head outside La Venta, Mexico (bottom, left); and a beautifully sculptured Mayan head (bottom, right).

the fourth to the tenth centuries A.D., the Mayas lived in that part of Mesoamerica now known as Guatemala. The other time span is the Late Period. During this time the Mayas migrated to the Yucatán and were conquered by the Spanish. Archaeologists speculate that the Mayas had accomplished great achievements in astronomy and mathematics as early as the fourth century B.C. Much is still to be discovered about the civilizations of the Mayas. In an attempt to rid the world of "pagan" influences, Spanish churchmen deliberately destroyed the Maya Codices. These are texts (set down in books written on bark paper) which contained the lore of the Mayas. Only three of these books escaped destruction by the Spanish conquerors. Fortunately, the Mayas also inscribed their texts on the many stone monuments which they built near the temples and palaces of their now abandoned "cities" or ceremonial centers.

The Mayas built their greatest centers in the tropical areas of Honduras, Belize, and Mexico's Yucatán. These were centers for religious ceremonies rather than cities to be lived in. Between 1839 and 1842, 44 ancient Mayan centers were found in Mexico and Central America. The best known are Copán in Honduras, Tikal, Uaxactún Pelenque, and Piedras Negras in present-day Guatemala, Yarchilán in Mexico, and Labná and Uxmal in Yucatán.

It was hard to keep the jungle cut back, so the great religious centers were made up of many pyramids and platforms. Small temples were atop the pyramids. Wide streets surrounded the main temple. Each Mayan center had a ball court for an early form of basketball and seats for spectators. In the rural areas, the people lived in thatch-roofed huts.

The principal god of the Mayan religion was Itzamna who was believed to be kind and good. Other important gods were Quetzalcoatl, the feathered serpent god; Chacmool, the sky, rain, and sun god; and Yum Kax, god of the harvest.

The Mayas were short and husky, with sloping foreheads, full lips, dark brown eyes, and long dark hair. The men wore a sleeveless jacket, loin cloth, and sandals. Women wore a skirt and shawl or simple long dress, but went barefoot except on long journeys when they wore sandals. Their cotton clothing was worn for personal adornment rather than for warmth because they lived in a tropical climate. They raised the cotton, spun it into thread and wove the cloth which they dyed bright colors with dyes made from berries.

The agricultural economy of the Mayas was based on corn or maize, which they cultivated as early as 2,000 B.C. Tending the *milpas,* or cornfields, was their most important daily activity. Corn was the staple food of the Mayas. They also raised potatoes, beans, onions, squash, pumpkins, tropical fruits, turkeys, and honeybees. They burned the trees and the vegetation of the jungle to obtain planting areas and waited for rain from the god, Chacmool. Then they sowed the seeds by hand and waited for the god, Yum Kax, to bring the crop. They had no tools other than stone axes; metal was not known until much later. Their constant chore was to keep the jungle from overrunning the land.

The Mayas have been called the "Greeks of the New World." These highly intelligent people were peaceful and religious. Their art does not show death, warfare, or destruction. They used an arithmetic system of dots and dashes which included the concept of zero. They were the only Indians to invent a true system of ideographic (or picture) writing.

Mayan civilization flourished from about 317 to 889 A.D. and was at its height between 731 and 810. The Mayas left their great southern centers (which had become cities) and moved northward into the Yucatán Peninsula. There they established a new empire which rose to even greater heights. The reason for their migration is unknown, but possibilities are volcano activity, civil war, change in climate, or invasion. This move hastened their destruction; they were attacked by hostile Indians from the Mexican plateau, and their culture declined until the Spanish finally conquered them in 1546.

Today there are 2,000,000 Mayas in Mexico, and slightly more than that number in Guatemala.

The Aztecs. The great civilization of the Aztec Indians was flourishing in Central America and Mexico by 1505 when Columbus anchored his ships in the Gulf of Honduras on his last voyage to America.

The Aztecs were a small wandering tribe which reached Mexico in about 1200. They conquered other tribes and, by the late 1400s, controlled all the land between the Gulf of Mexico and the Pacific Ocean.

According to legend, the chief Aztec god, Huitzilopochtli, god of sun and war, told his people that they should settle on the spot where they saw an eagle perched on a cactus eating a snake held in its talons. Legend says this is why Tenochtitlán, the capital city of the Aztecs (now Mexico City) was built in 1325 on some small islands in the middle of Lake Texcoco. The Aztecs built huge rafts, covered them with earth, and, thus, had floating farmlands. On these *chinampas* ("floating gardens") they grew maize and vegetables. Eventually roots from the tree rafts attached themselves to the bottom of the shallow lake to become permanent foundations for buildings. In this way the city grew until by 1440, under Montezuma I, it was the major city of the Aztecs. By the sixteenth century this canal-laced city had plaster buildings, gardens, and pyramid-like temples to the gods. It was a great fortress with drawbridges connected to shore, and it housed over 100,000 people.

The Aztecs grew maize, beans, and peppers both for home consumption and for trade. Their homes, like those of the Mayas, were thatch-roofed huts. Their clothing was made of roughly woven cotton. From the agave or century plant they made strong thread and an alcoholic beverage, called *pulque*. They also drank chocolate and ate avocados, pineapples, squash, fish, turkeys, geese, and ducks.

By the time the Aztecs had established themselves in Tenochtitlán, decisions governing the society were being made by the twenty or so tribal chiefs. In 1376 A.D., the entire population was structured so that each person was assigned a specific role. At the top of the social structure were the nobles who claimed their positions through heredity. At the bottom were the slaves, who were usually prisoners of war. As the Aztecs became more successful in battle and their empire grew, their rulers became more autocratic. By the time the Spanish arrived in Mexico in 1519, the Aztec emperor, Montezuma II, was considered and treated as a living god.

In order to fully understand the Aztecs, it is necessary to examine their religious beliefs. To the Aztecs the world was an unhappy place. When a child was born into a family, there was a ritual performed in which the mid-wife chanted about life as full of "sorrow, weeping, and suffering." The Aztecs believed that death and destruction were inevitable and that the gods enjoyed warfare among men. To remain in favor with the gods the Aztecs waged war against their neighbors with the purpose of taking prisoners to be used as human sacrifices. These captives were stretched over a stone altar called a *techcatl*, their chests were opened by an obsidian blade, and the heart was removed. The heart was placed in a bowl and left out in the sun. Within a brief time the blood had dried, proving to the Aztecs that the gods' thirst had been satisfied. Because the Aztecs could never be sure of satisfying the gods, it was necessary to sacrifice more victims. It has been estimated that as many as 20,000 persons were sacrificed by the Aztecs each year to please the gods.

The Spanish conquest of the Aztec Empire, beginning in 1519, is one of the greatest accomplishments in human history. There is no doubt, however, that to a large extent, the success of Hernán Cortés must be attributed to a strange historical coincidence. To the Aztec people the god Quetzalcoatl was special. Translated, the name means "plumed serpent." This god was frequently depicted as a reptile with the feathered coverings of the quetzal bird. Of all the Aztec gods, Quetzalcoatl was the only one ever idealized as a human figure. All Aztecs, including their emperors, considered Quetzalcoatl as the original ruler and that one day, he "would return out of the waters of the east, as a bearded man riding on an animal (the horse)" to again occupy his seat on the throne. Aztec astrologers had also calculated that the god would return at the exact time that Cortés landed with his expedition out of the waters of the east—from Cuba.

When reports of Cortés' arrival reached Emperor Montezuma's ears, there was no doubt that Quetzalcoatl had returned to claim his position of leadership. By 1521, the conquest of the Aztec Empire was complete and the Spanish began a rule which lasted almost 300 years.

Today there are over 1,000,000 people throughout Mexico who speak dialects of the Aztec language.

The Incas.   These Indians lived in the mountains of Peru. The Incas built great temples to their gods from stone blocks that were cut and fitted together with great skill and accuracy without cement or any other material. The fit was so perfect that a knife blade could not be inserted into the spaces between the blocks. Their capital city—Cuzco—was built in this way.

In 1911, an American explorer, Hiram Bingham, discovered Machu Picchu, about 50 miles northwest of Cuzco. This city, hidden from the Spaniards, contains beautiful stone structures which are the ruins of Machu Picchu. The city was built 6,750 feet above sea level and is one of the most fascinating sites in the Western Hemisphere.

The Incas built up an empire in western South America and went on to conquer other Indians. They spread their civilization far beyond Peru to Colombia, Ecuador, Bolivia, and northern regions of Argentina and Chile. At its peak the empire included perhaps 16 million people. The Incas maintained control over their vast holdings because of their superb ability to organize and govern. They moved inhabitants out of newly conquered lands and resettled them in areas containing loyal tribes, or sent loyal tribes to settle conquered land.

The Incas were farmers who grew cotton, potatoes, maize, peanuts, squash, tomatoes, and beans. They built irrigation systems in the coastal deserts, and they cut terraces to increase cultivation on the high mountain slopes. These Indians also

CASE INQUIRY: A View of the Incas

The Indian civilizations of Latin America had developed advanced social, economic, and political systems long before the arrival of the Europeans. The following excerpt also reveals the origin of the European name for the Inca's homeland.

> The name Peru was not known to the natives...it signifies *river,* a word which, pronounced by one of the natives, in answer to a question put by the Spaniards, led to the error causing this name to be given to the vast empire of the Incas. The troops of Pizarro believed that the inhabitants called the country Peru.
>
> Roads to the four provinces started from Cuzco, the capital or center of the Peruvian monarchy. At the head of each province was a viceroy, or governor, who ruled with the aid of one or more counselors. Each province was divided into...departments...according to the number of inhabitants. And for the better administration and easier inspection..., the Incas invented a simple system of subdivision. The population of the country was divided into groups of ten, each under the command of a *decurion:* ten decurions obeyed one *centurion:* ten centurions, or one thousand inhabitants, had...a principal magistrate, and one hundred decurions...formed a department under a governor.
>
> In cultivating the earth, they always followed a fixed rule; first were cultivated the lands pertaining to the protecting divinity. Afterward they attended to the lands of the aged, the sick, the widowed, and the orphans, also to those of the soldiers who were engaged in active service, whose wives were looked upon as widows. After this, the people cultivated their own lands, ... but under an obligation to aid his neighbor, ... a fraternal custom which even at this day is practiced by the Peruvian Indians.
>
> The distribution of the nation, ... possessed many advantages: it facilitated the administration of the whole country, ... gave it a unity ... and secured an exact account of the increase or diminution of the population. By the equal distribution of the land, the Incas avoided pauperism (poverty). ...

1. Describe the evidence we have that the Incas had a highly efficient system of political administration.

2. Explain whether or not you believe the Inca system of land distribution to be a good system? Can you think of a modern day system that is similar?

From a reappraisal of the Incas by Mariano Educardo de Riviero, 1851, originally written in Spanish.

The power and majesty of the Incan civilization can be seen at the site of the ancient fortress Machu Picchu in Peru.

domesticated the alpaca and llama and developed various industries such as spinning and weaving of cotton and wool, metal work, pottery making, and gold mining. Unlike the Mayas, the Incas had no writing system, yet they kept records by using a series of strings tied to a belt to indicate the number of items received or delivered.

Authority was centered in the Lord Inca (the ruler) who had absolute power over the lives of his people from birth to death. He was thought to be the Child of the Sun and was worshipped as a god. He was also the emperor, whose wishes were enforced by the priests and other officials. The emperor supervised the cultivation of crops and distributed the land. Individual land ownership was prohibited, but each family was allotted an adequate plot of land which was enlarged as the family grew.

Inca officials forced people to live in districts and selected occupations for them. They were constantly supervised and regulated; there was no freedom. This system resulted in people who completely lacked self-reliance but were obedient and loyal.

The Spanish, whose appetite for gold and silver was stimulated by the vast treasures of Mexico, grew even more greedy when they heard about the enormous wealth of the Inca. In 1532, Francisco Pizarro was able to land a small expedition in

Peru to begin the conquest. Like Cortés, Pizarro's arrival was marked by fortunate circumstance. The Inca, Huayna Capac, had died in 1525, and the empire was divided between his two sons. Within a short time the brothers engaged in civil war, thus dividing the leadership and weakening the empire. In the struggle, Atahualpa emerged victorious.

Atahualpa had little time to enjoy his victory. The Spanish, led by the fearless Pizarro, won a great victory over the Inca at the battle of Cajamarca, and Atahualpa was captured. Atahualpa made a bid for freedom by appealing to their greed. He offered Pizarro a storehouse of gold and silver in exchange for his release. The ransom offer was agreed to and fulfilled. The Spanish, however, did not keep their word, and the emperor was executed. The conquest of the remaining Inca Empire was easily completed in 1535.

B. THE EUROPEANS EXPLORE AND CONQUER

The Crusades, which started in Europe in the 11th century, brought about a gradual change in the thinking of Europeans. The Crusaders learned that the East had much to offer the West. Upon returning to Europe from the East, they brought back such products as exotic, rare perfume, which was highly prized in an era when few people bathed; spices, which were used to preserve food; drugs, which were used to relieve pain; silk, velvet, rugs, jewels, and rare foods, especially fruit. The demand created in Europe for these eastern goods increased trade. This expanded trade led to the growth of towns and cities in Europe which, in turn, provided the opportunity for people to meet each other and exchange ideas. Curiosity was encouraged during the period of the European Renaissance. When the printing press was invented in about 1450, more people became informed, for more printed material was readily available.

The importing and exporting of eastern products became a monopoly of the Italian city-states. The determination of European business leaders to smash this monopoly led to explorations to find a direct all-water route to the East, preferably by a northwest passage. Other reasons for exploration included the desire to find gold and silver, to claim new lands for one's country, and, for many, to satisfy the spirit of adventure in strange new lands.

During the 15th century, Portuguese navigators sailed down the western coast of Africa for short distances, venturing further each time. Prince Henry "the Navigator" of Portugal had established a school to teach sailors knowledge of the sea in order to eliminate their fear and superstition. He hoped that his navigators would find a new route to the East around Africa. In 1488 Bartholomew Díaz sailed around the southern tip of Africa but turned back. In 1498 Vasco da Gama made the complete voyage around Africa, sailed cross the Indian Ocean, and reached the west coast of India.

Spain was jealous of Portugal's leadership in exploration. In Spain's employ, Italian sailors set sail to find an all-water northwest passage to the East. One of them, Christopher Columbus, sailed west, hoping to reach Asia. After two months at sea, he sighted the Bahamas on October 12, 1492. Fifteen days later he discovered Cuba, which he believed to be Japan. He next discovered the island of Hispañola. Pope Alexander VI granted Ferdinand and Isabella of Spain exclusive rights over the newly discovered land. The Pope laid down an imaginary line 100 leagues (about 300 miles) west of the Azores. All discoveries west of this line would belong to Spain. In 1494 Portugal and Spain shifted the line 270 leagues to the west by the Treaty of Tordesillas; by this agreement Portugal claimed Brazil, which was discovered in 1500 by Cabral.

In 1513 Vasco Nuñez de Balboa marched west across Panama, and sighted the Pacific Ocean. Ponce de León, a veteran of Columbus' voyages, was Puerto Rico's first explorer, settler, and governor in 1508. In 1513, acting on a rumor of a wonderful "fountain of youth," he sailed to the north-northeast, where he discovered several other islands of the Bahamas, as well as Florida.

On the mainland, other *conquistadores* were moving at a

faster pace—for it was there that they thought they would find El Dorado, the legendary city of gold.

In 1519, the Aztec ruler of Mexico, Montezuma, sent his ambassadors to meet with Cortés somewhere along the Tabasco Coast. Included among the gifts delivered to Cortés, who was thought to be the returning god Quetzalcoatl, were golden objects in the form of shields, sceptres, and war bonnets. It was these treasures that encouraged the Spaniard's desire for even more gold and silver. By 1521, Cortés had marched on Montezuma's capital and destroyed it. Tenochtitlán (present-day Mexico City) was sacked of its treasures and its population was massacred; Mexico was thus added to the Spanish empire.

The Inca Empire was stronger and richer than the Aztec Empire and stretched down the western coast of South America. Attracted by stories of vast gold and silver mines, Francisco Pizarro entered the area. In 1533, Pizarro and his soldiers murdered the Indian emperor and conquered the Incas. So much gold and silver was sent to Spain from Peru and Mexico that a gold rush developed in the Americas. Great numbers of Spaniards left their homes and families to seek gold in the New World. Gold seekers under the leadership of Hernando de Soto explored what is now the southeastern section of the United States. The southwestern part was explored by Francisco Coronado. Neither expedition found gold in America but Spain's empire in the New World increased. De Soto later discovered the Mississippi River.

The first man to sail around the Western Hemisphere was Portuguese Ferdinand Magellan who sailed for the Spanish king. He sailed on a southwestward course from Spain. In 1519, he sailed around the southern part of South America and then set a northwestward course straight across the Pacific. Magellan was killed in the Philippine Islands and only one of his five ships reached home—the first to sail around the world.

With its possessions in the Americas and elsewhere, Spain enlarged its empire to such an extent that it became the leading world power of the 16th century.

QUESTIONS AND ACTIVITIES

KEY WORDS, PEOPLE, AND PHRASES

Can you explain or identify the following words and names? Use an encyclopedia if necessary.

Ice Age	Tenochtitlán	Crusades
maize	Montezuma II	*conquistadores*
alpaca	Atahualpa	Magellan
Yucatán	Huascar	Yucatán
Pizarro	autocratic	Cortés
Mesoamerica		

MULTIPLE CHOICE TEST

In each of the following you have four possible answer choices. Select the only correct answer.

1. Which best describes the reason why the Mayas built their great religious centers on platforms? *(a)* Floods were common in their area. *(b)* They were afraid of jungle animals. *(c)* It was hard to keep the jungle cut back. *(d)* They showed great respect for their gods.

2. The "Maya Codices," were *(a)* secret messages to the Inca emperor, *(b)* books on Maya folklore, *(c)* Mayan knives, *(d)* religious songs of the Spanish.

3. The stone altar used by the Aztecs to sacrifice their victims was called *(a)* techantl, *(b)* roca, *(c)* Tenochtitlán, *(d)* maize.

4. The legend of the eagle and the snake is associated with the *(a)* Mayas, *(b)* Incas, *(c)* Chibchas, *(d)* Aztecs.

5. The chief characteristic of the Aztec religion was *(a)* human sacrifice, *(b)* animal worship, *(c)* donations of food, *(d)* worship of one god.

6. The Aztec Empire was conquered by *(a)* De Soto, *(b)* Pizarro, *(c)* Cortez, *(d)* Coronado.

7. The Inca Indians lived in the mountains of *(a)* Mexico, *(b)* Peru, *(c)* El Salvador, *(d)* Nicaragua.

8. One difference between the Incas and Mayas was that the Incas had no *(a)* writing system, *(b)* knowledge of corn growing, *(c)* domesticated animals, *(d)* primitive industries.

9. Which of the following explains why the Spanish conquest of the Inca Empire was swift and easily completed? *(a)* Span-

ish soldiers were better fighters. (b) The Indians ran out of food. (c) The Spanish killed the Indian leaders. (d) The Spanish had better weapons.

10. Quetzalcoatl, which means "plumed serpent," was (a) an Inca warrior, (b) the emperor of the Aztec people, (c) an important Aztec god, (d) the name for Cortés.

11. The complete voyage around Africa to India was first made by (a) Bartholomew Díaz, (b) Prince Henry "the Navigator," (c) Ferdinand Magellan, (d) Vasco da Gama.

12. The Papal demarcation line divided the New World between (a) Italy and France, (b) Spain and Portugal, (c) Spain and Italy, (d) Portugal and France.

13. Ponce de León was the first European to discover what came to be called (a) Mexico, (b) Puerto Rico, (c) Florida, (d) Bermuda.

14. Which of the following built the strongest and richest empire in the Americas? (a) Incas, (b) Mayas, (c) Aztecs.

15. The first man to command a sailing expedition around the world was (a) Pizarro, (b) Magellan, (c) Cortés, (d) De Soto.

THINGS TO DO

1. Prepare a series of posters tracing the development of Indian civilizations in Latin America.

2. Present an oral report on the importance of Indian contributions to agriculture.

3. Research project: Trace the reasons why the outnumbered Spanish explorers found it easy to conquer the Indians of Latin America.

4. Draw a map of Latin America and on it color the centers of Maya, Inca, and Aztec civilizations.

5. Draw a rough sketch indicating what you would display on the cover of a book on Latin America.

6. Prepare a detailed report on the explorations of either Cortés, Pizarro, or Cabral.

7. Write an original essay on how you think people came to the Americas.

8. Present a report on everyday life in an Inca village.

9. Pretend you are a newspaper reporter and write a news article on the conquistadores.

10. In committee, prepare a group report on contributions Indians have made to life today.

3

THE MOVEMENTS FOR INDEPENDENCE

A. THE COLONIAL PERIOD UNDER SPAIN AND PORTUGAL

Spain and Portugal ruled empires in America for a period longer than three centuries. The forms of imperial administration contrasted sharply between the two powers. Portugal's governing of Brazil was somewhat loose and ill defined; Spain's colonial rule was very tightly structured. At the top of the Spanish power structure was the monarch, the king or queen.

To understand Spanish colonial rule in the Americas one must first understand the philosophical base upon which the monarch ruled. In Spain, it was believed that the monarch ruled in the best interests of the people. It was understood that the monarch's rule was fair, "Christian," and just. Under these circumstances, it was reasoned, the monarch was able to demand loyalty from the people.

This view of royal authority laid the foundation for absolute monarchy by the Spanish ruler in the name of justice. The monarch was left to determine the best interests of the people, limited only by the laws of God and nature. Nor was the ruler restricted by a written constitution or custom in carrying out his or her office. The will of the monarch became the highest source of law.

This concept of royal authority was accepted in the Spanish colonies. Over the 300 years of Spanish rule in the Americas, the right of the Crown to rule was never seriously challenged.

Within this political framework, the powers of the ruler's colonial administrators in the New World had a direct relation-

44

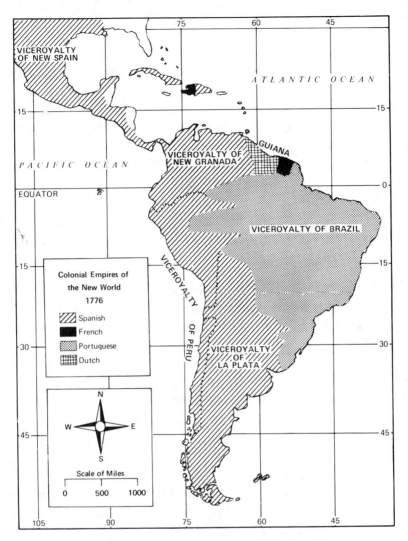

Labels on map:

VICEROYALTY OF NEW SPAIN

ATLANTIC OCEAN

15

PACIFIC OCEAN

VICEROYALTY OF NEW GRANADA

GUIANA

EQUATOR

0

VICEROYALTY OF BRAZIL

VICEROYALTY OF PERU

Colonial Empires of
the New World
1776

Spanish
French
Portuguese
Dutch

VICEROYALTY OF LA PLATA

N
W   E
S

Scale of Miles
0   500   1000

COLONIAL EMPIRES IN THE NEW WORLD

ship to the ability to influence royal action. The great distance between Spain and the colonies and the limitations of time on correspondence gave greater flexibility in implementing royal decrees. It became accepted practice by these officials to acknowledge the monarch's authority while "bending" laws to suit the local situation. The monarch, in order to control the situation from distant Spain, appointed only those officials in whom he or she held the highest trust.

45

Mercantilism. Royalist policy, be it Spanish or Portuguese, was based on *mercantilism*: the economic idea that the colonies were to provide the mother country with those products not available in Europe and maintain a favorable trade balance in commercial dealings. The colonies were forbidden to manufacture any products that would compete with industry in Spain or Portugal. The colonizing countries became rich while the colonies remained underdeveloped and dependent on imports. Except for minor industries such as pottery, weaving, and tanning, little opportunity was provided for the development of artisan industry.

The Powerful Peninsulares. Because of mercantilism, the Spanish and Portuguese colonies in the Americas remained economically backwards. In addition, opportunities for advancement were denied to the majority of the peoples living in the colonies in the early years of the 19th century. The dominant group were known as *peninsulares,* or those who had been born on the Iberian peninsula which consisted of Spain and Portugal. The *peninsulares* were always given preference and access to the highest positions in the Americas. For example, a total of 170 viceroys (representatives of the monarch) served the Crown during colonial rule. Only four of them were not *peninsulares.* There were approximately 602 governors who administered royal territory. Only fourteen were not *peninsulares.* Indeed, a hotly debated political question in both Spain and Portugal was the extent to which the non native-born European was fit to govern!

Meanwhile, the *criollo,* the American-born Spanish, were discontented under the restrictions which denied them power and prestige. Higher political offices and economic success were reserved for the *peninsulares.* Competition, resentment, and later, rivalry, characterized the relations between these two white groups. The *peninsulares* struggled to maintain their favored position while the *criollos* sought ways to change the situation. They even started to think of themselves not as "Spanish," but rather, as "Americans." Combined, the *penin-*

sulares and *criollos* formed a total of only 20 percent of the population, which by 1800 was estimated at 15 million. The balance of people in the lands controlled by Spain and Portugal were *mestizos.* These were the offspring of unions between the Spanish and Indians. *Mulattoes,* the offspring of blacks brought from Africa as slaves and Europeans, were another group.

Each of these groups had reason to despise colonial rule. On the other hand, they had no great love for those who wanted to replace the *peninsulares.* The *mestizos,* the product of two cultures, were embittered over their rejection by both. The Indians worked for others on a land that was once theirs. To the blacks in bondage, the end of imperial rule offered a hope for freedom and a chance to carve a place for themselves in a new society. In fact, when the wars for independence began, the focus of struggle lay between *criollo and royalist.* In some cases, the resentment of Indians against *criollos* caused them to rally to the imperial banner as hostilities began.

The Seeds of Independence.   Despite the general success of 300 years of Spanish and Portuguese rule, the end of imperial control was inevitable. Mention has already been made of the frustrations of the *criollo.* In addition, there were external influences which helped to shape the independence movement. In Europe, a part of the world where both *peninsulare* and *criollo* looked for cultural enrichment, the liberal ideas of the Enlightenment had taken hold. Intellectuals in the colonies were provoked by the philosophy which urged reason and challenged fixed ways of thought and action. These liberal ideas had to some extent been successfully tested in revolutions first, in the United States, and later, in France.

The event that sparked the independence movement in Spanish America came in 1808. In that year Napoleon invaded Spain and replaced the king with his brother, Joseph Bonaparte. The unifying symbol of the monarch was gone. With this link broken, all of the grievances and discontent emerged. The colonial peoples waited only for leadership to sever the remaining bond of occupation.

B. THE WARS FOR INDEPENDENCE

Throughout Latin America. most of the actual fighting was done between the years 1810 and 1824. In 1804, however, Haitian independence had already been achieved as the black islanders rallied, first under Toussaint L'Ouverture, and then under Jean-Jacques Dessalines, who succeeded in ousting the French. Haiti became only the second nation in the hemisphere to gain its independence. A dozen years later, Simón Bolívar sailed from Haiti in his quest to drive the Spanish from America. Among all of the military leaders who played a role in the South American independence movement, the two most widely acclaimed are Simón Bolívar and José de San Martín. Their personalities differed and their styles of behavior contrasted sharply. Bolívar was a man of passion and emotion with a flair for the dramatic. San Martín, on the other hand, was humble and modest. Whatever their personal differences, Spanish-America could not have had two more bold or brilliant generals.

While Simón Bolivar (left) fought for freedom in the northern regions of Latin America, José de San Martin (right) helped liberate the south.

From the two extremes of the continent, Bolívar in the north and San Martín in the south, rebel armies went forth to secure the independence of America from Spanish rule. The struggle was not an easy one especially for Bolívar. His troops suffered terrible defeats before his armies emerged victorious. Over a period of almost fourteen years, Bolívar won freedom for Venezuela, Colombia, Ecuador, Peru, and Bolivia. From liberated Argentina, San Martín joined Bernardo O'Higgins to defeat the Spanish before moving northward to Peru. By 1824, active Spanish resistance came to an end as an allied army defeated the Spanish in the battle of Ayacucho.

Mexican Independence. In Mexico, 1810 was also the year that marked the beginning of movement against Spanish rule. Following the overthrow of Spain's rightful monarch by the French in 1808, the Mexican *criollos* seized the opportunity to transfer power from the *peninsulares* into their own hands. The *peninsulares* managed to regain control and jailed the *criollo* leaders. One *criollo* leader who managed to escape was a parish priest named Father Miguel Hidalgo. In September of 1810, in the little town of Dolores in central Mexico, Father Hidalgo rang the church bell in his now famous *"grito de Dolores"* or call for Mexican independence. Father Hidalgo's movement had a different thrust than the mere expulsion of *peninsulares* from power. Hidalgo was interested in a total reformation of government and society. His social program was more than the *criollos* could accept and within a year he was captured and executed. Hidalgo's banner was taken up by yet another priest, José María Morelos, who after some early success was also captured and executed by Spanish forces. With the death of Morelos, the hopes for social improvements in the lives of the *mestizos* and Indians were dashed and Mexico lapsed back into colonial status. When independence came to Mexico in 1821, it resulted from an agreement between *peninsulares* and *criollos* to support a soldier who had fought against the patriots Hidalgo and Morelos. His name was Augustín

Iturbide. After proclaiming himself emperor, Iturbide was forced to abdicate within a year. Mexico then became a republic.

Brazil Breaks Away from Portugal. In Brazil, independence was gained without the shedding of blood. The actors differed only in name. In colonial Brazil the power struggle was between *mazombos* (American-born Portuguese) and *reinols,* Europeans who came to America from Portugal. Again, it was Napolean's invasion of Portugal in 1808 and the evacuation of the royal family to Brazil that made the event possible. After ruling from Rio de Janeiro for some thirteen years, the royal court returned to Portugal. They left behind a prince named Pedro to serve as regent. Pedro came under the influence of nationalist mind-ed *mazambos,* and in 1822, declared Brazilian independent and was crowned emperor.

Thus, by 1825, all of the Latin American territories except for Cuba and Puerto Rico had won independence from Spanish and Portuguese colonial rule. By 1898, these two islands would become independent following the Spanish-American War.

Despite strong attempts by many Latin American governments to integrate the Indian into the national culture, the Indian continues to resist assimilation choosing to maintain cultural practices including Indian costume.

Daniel J. Mugan

CASE INQUIRY: Brazil's Constitution of 1824

In 1824, Brazil drafted a constitution providing for the three traditional branches of government and the *poder moderador*— the powers of the emperor Pedro.

Title V—Of the Emperor.
Chapter I—*Of the Moderating Power*

Article 98. The Moderating Power is the key to the entire political organization and it is delegated exclusively to the Emperor as the Supreme Chief of the Nation and its First Representative so that he constantly can watch over the maintenance of the independence, equilibrium, and harmony of the other Political Powers.

Article 99. The Person of the Emperor is inviolable and sacred. He is not subject to any responsibility.

Article 100. His titles are "Constitutional Emperor and Perpetual Defender of Brazil" and he should be addressed as Imperial Majesty.

Article 101. The Emperor exercises the Moderating Power.
1. By naming Senators.
2. By convoking the General Assembly between sessions when the good of the Empire demands it.
3. By sanctioning the Decrees and Resolutions of the General Assembly. . . .
5. By postponing or adjourning the General Assembly and by dissolving the Chamber of Deputies in those cases in which the well-being of the State requires it; by convoking immediately another to substitute for it.
6. By naming and freely dismissing the Ministers of State....
8. By paroling and by moderating the penalties imposed on criminals condemned by sentence.
9. By conceding amnesty in urgent cases or when counseled by humanity and the good of the State.

1. From this brief excerpt, how can you show that **Brazil** had a highly centralized form of government?
2. In what ways does this constitution reflect the ideals and practices of Europeon governments in the 19th century?

From a translation of *Constituicao Politica do Imperio do Brazil*. Impressao de Joao Nunes Esteves, Lisbon, Portugal, 1826.

51

C. THE DIFFICULT PROCESS OF DEVELOPMENT

The revolutionary movements towards independence were generally conservative in nature. They were not aimed at reversing the basic structure of society. The disappearance of the imperial system, with all of its defects, left a vacuum in Latin America. The new governments attempted to fill this vacuum in a number of makeshift ways. Having had no tradition of democratic practices and only limited experiences in self-government through *cabildos* (town councils), the political leaders of the newly independent nations began to look about in the hope of finding a formula for success. Inspired by the ideas of the French Revolution and impressed by the brilliant constitution of the United States, the Latin American republics wrote their own constitutions. These documents reflected the noblest of ideals. Unfortunately, the new constitutions had little relevance to the reality of life in the republics. Perhaps for that reason, the writing and rewriting of constitutions became common practice. In less than one century, Bolivia had ten constitutions, Venezuela eleven, and Ecuador twelve!

Furthermore, the minority elite, sometimes known as the *oligarchy,* had no interest in promoting the ideas of democracy for the masses of *mestizos,* Indians, and blacks who lived in the new nations. In the 19th century in Latin America, political rivalry existed between liberals, who were usually urban, business leaders and professionals, and conservatives, who were rural and enjoyed large landholdings. Political debate frequently revolved around the role of the Church and its power rather than the condition of the masses. Usually, the liberals sought checks on the Church and access to its great wealth while the conservatives championed the position of the Church.

The Power of the Church. As for the Catholic Church, with some exceptions, it supported the status quo. In the 19th century, the Church, always more conservative in the Americas than elsewhere, counseled acceptance and humility to its faithful. The Church taught that despite the rigors of this world, things

Guerrilla armies have been challenging the governments of Central American countries for the past decade, similar to the guerrilla movement which brought Fidel Castro to power in Cuba.

would be better in the next life. This became a sustaining message to those who could hope for few economic and social advances. Because the Church was rich from grants and money gifts, it probably had less interest in the missionary activities of the earlier centuries. Church leaders were more concerned over the administration and management of their considerable wealth. There are frequent examples of close family links between the Church hierarchy and the conservative elite. Despite resentment of Church wealth, power, and prestige, there was no thought of attacking Church teaching. Rather there was an intense desire to control its position and functions in society.

The Caudillo and the Military. The lack of national unity and the great geographic obstacles of distance and rough terrain combined with a weak political tradition and inexperience were formidable problems for Latin American rulers to overcome. As a result, politics was marked by violence. Chaos, power struggles, and changes in government were common. Democratic elections were rare. In this continuing vacuum new factors emerged in the attempt to bring order and stability. Two of these were the *caudillo,* or strong man, and the military.

The *caudillo,* or dictator, a tradition which continues in present-day Latin America, ruled with little opposition and usually maintained the status quo with a firm hand. The legitimacy of *caudillo* rule was never widely accepted, however, and his power depended upon how well he protected his own position. Because *caudillo* rule was largely personal, his death or removal from office meant the end of his influence.

The military, on the other hand, found themselves in an unusual position. The absence of effective political institutions and traditions caused them to play the role of protectors of domestic order. They also helped bring about change of government. Aware of the mighty force represented by the army, Latin American leaders attempted to gain support by rewarding the officers with handsome salaries and other benefits. Those who tried to cut down on wasteful military budgets were frequently overthrown and replaced by someone more sympathetic to the army's interests.

The political instability throughout Latin America in the years following independence had a harmful impact upon economic development. As the 19th century progressed, however, it became clear that there were two sectors upon which prosperity relied—the sector devoted to local consumption and the sector devoted to mining natural resources for export. By the end of the century, stability was accompanied by a boom in economic development. Markets opened up in Europe and elsewhere for Latin America's crops and minerals. As foreign investment poured capital into the new nations, immigration from the Old World began. The European immigrants had a great impact on the Latin American countries, especially those in the southern part of the continent. All of these factors combined to spur urbanization and industrialization.

QUESTIONS AND ACTIVITIES

KEY WORDS, PEOPLE, AND PHRASES

Can you define or identify the following words and names? Use an encyclopedia or dictionary if necessary.

absolute monarchy   *criollos*   Father Hidalgo
constitution   status quo   mulatto
colony   Simón Bolívar   national integration
mercantilism   Jóse de San Martín   urbanization
Enlightenment   Bernardo O'Higgins   *caudillo*
peninsulares   José María Morelos   oligarchy

MULTIPLE CHOICE TEST

In each of the following you have four possible choices. Select the only correct answer.

1. Under the economic theory of mercantilism, colonies exist for the benefit of *(a)* European nations, *(b)* Western Hemisphere nations, *(c)* the people of the colonies. *(d)* the mother country.
2. Which usually provides a country with a favorable balance of trade? *(a)* importing more than exporting, *(b)* exporting more than importing, *(c)* high tariffs, *(d)* low tariffs.
3. The economic development of the Spanish colonies gave rise to a spirit of *(a)* contentment, *(b)* obedience, *(c)* friendship, *(d)* rebellion.
4. The Latin American independence movement started in *(a)* Mexico, *(b)* Venezuela, *(c)* Haiti, *(d)* Argentina.
5. The Spanish empire in America lasted *(a)* 100 years, *(b)* 300 years, *(c)* 500 years, *(d)* it continues today.
6. The viceroy was *(a)* a representative of the monarch, *(b)* a high official of the Church, *(c)* a Latin American revolutionary, *(d)* a family title.
7. A person born in Latin America of Spanish parentage was called *(a)* zambo, *(b)* criollo, *(c)* mestizo, *(d)* royalist.
8. Simón Bolívar was the hero of the north but the hero of the south was *(a)* Bernardo O'Higgins, *(b)* Francisco Miranda, *(c)* Father Hidalgo, *(d)* José de San Martín.
9. José de San Martín aided the cause of freedom in *(a)* Venezuela, *(b)* Ecuador, *(c)* Argentina, *(d)* Mexico.

10. During the Latin American wars for independence, most of the battles took place between the years *(a)* 1776-1783, *(b)* 1801-1810, *(c)* 1810-1824, *(d)* 1898-1903.

11. The first revolution in New Spain was led by *(a)* Simón Bolívar, *(b)* Jóse de San Martín, *(c)* Father Hidalgo, *(d)* Bernnardo O'Higgins.

12. Haiti's fight for independence from France was led by *(a)* Joseph Napoleon, *(b)* Simón Bolívar, *(c)* Toussaint L'Ouverture, *(d)* Francisco Pizarro.

13. By 1825, all of Latin America was free of European rule except for *(a)* Mexico and Panama, *(b)* Cuba and Puerto Rico, *(c)* Cuba and Santo Domingo, *(d)* Chile and Costa Rica.

14. An elite is another name for *(a)* a rare tropical disease, *(b)* a powerful political party, *(c)* a powerful minority group, *(d)* an ancient Indian artifact.

15. Strong leaders who emerged in Latin America following the wars for independence were called *(a)* machos, *(b)* caudillos, *(c)* elites, *(d)* the liberals.

ESSAY QUESTIONS

1. Compare and contrast the colonial rule of Spain and Portugal in Latin America. What were the chief goals or aims of each European mother country? How successful were they in achieving their goals?

2. How can Latin America's colonial experiences explain the problems of political and economic development since independence? Do any Latin American countries reflect their colonial administrations? Give examples to support your position.

3. To what extent is a person's position in Latin America influenced by race, income, and religion? If you were a Latin American, how would you try to better your position in society?

4. Select *two* great Latin American leaders—one historical figure and one present leader—and describe the qualities that make them admirable.

5. Many historians believe that the independence movements in Latin America did not improve the life of the people in the region. Using the independence movement in Mexico as an example, show how the historians are *correct* in their assessment.

THINGS TO DO

1. Prepare a chart of colonial uprisings against Spain. Include countries, leaders, and battles.
2. Present a report explaining why the soldiers of Spain could not stop the colonial rebels.
3. Prepare a map of the Western Hemisphere showing Spanish possessions before and after the colonial wars.
4. Research paper: The American Revolutionary War had a tremendous effect on Latin America.
5. Debate the topic: *Resolved*—Spain did more good in Latin America than bad.
6. Write to the consulates of Argentina, Venezuela, and Chile. Ask for information on their leaders in the Latin America independence movement. Prepare brief biographical descriptions of these leaders.
7. Write a short essay on the advantages and disadvantages of the economic theory of mercantilism.

4

THE PEOPLE
AND THEIR CULTURE

A. THE PEOPLE

According to one noted historian, the *conquistadores* came to the New World seeking "gold, glory, and God." It is true enough that the early explorers were driven by the lure of gold, relished the glory of conquest, and felt a sincere obligation to convert people to their faith. Certainly the tales about America told in Spain and Portugal by the early explorers influenced countless young Iberians. The romantic appeal of a far-off and exotic land, the chance to earn a fortune in gold, and the hope to live out one's days as a respected gentleman had enormous appeal.

Thus, when the *conquistadores* came to America, they had no intention to work the land, settle, and establish a new life. Because they never planned to remain in the New World, the *conquistadores* left their wives and families behind in the "Old World." Those who remained married Indian women. From this intermingling of blood a new group was created, the *mestizos*. The *mestizos* now make up most of the total population of South America, especially in Bolivia, Brazil, Chile, Colombia, Paraguay, and Venezuela. They are the leaders of Latin America. Teachers, doctors, scientists, lawyers, generals, and even presidents of countries are likely to be *mestizos*. Later, when Africans arrived in large numbers as slaves, yet another group was added to the mix. There came into being *mulattoes, zambos,* and *quadroons*. Many Portuguese intermarried with the Indians and black slaves. Their descendants have had a strong influence on Brazilian culture. Blacks are also a strong influence in Cuba, Puerto Rico, the Dominican Republic, Panama, Jamaica, Trinidad, Guyana, and Haiti.

In the late 19th century, millions of Europeans emigrated to Latin America especially to Brazil, Argentina, and Uruguay. They gave that region the varied ethnic and racial mix that we know today. As early as 1925, a well known Mexican writer, Vasconcelos, began using the term *La Raza Cosmica* to describe the fusion of Europeans, Amerindians, and Africans inhabiting the region. Vasconcelos believed that this new "cosmic race" would not only spell the end of racial differences but would result in a new civilization for all mankind.

The perception of race in Latin America is unique. In Latin America greater recognition is given to the variety of physical and cultural groupings and terms are employed accordingly. As a result, words have a cultural significance that go beyond racial meaning. Even Spanish colonial law made provision for the "person of color" to purchase or otherwise obtain "whiteness." In Latin America one is an "Indian" to the extent that he or she chooses to dress, speak a native American language, or perform that role in society. If that same individual moves to a large city and changes his or her life style, the individual loses identity as "Indian." As an individual advances in terms of education, social, or occupational status, his or her skin color becomes less important. It is not, on the other hand, a correct assumption that no prejudice based on color exists in Latin America.

B. LANGUAGES, CUSTOMS, AND EDUCATION

Languages. While Spanish is the language spoken by most of the people in Latin America, it is not the same kind of Spanish that is spoken in Spain. Some Latin Americans use another word to describe their style of Spanish and that word is *castellano*. Spanish, or *el español,* they point out correctly, is spoken in Spain. Indeed, the intonation and accents that are used in speaking Latin American Spanish and the addition of words from other languages seems to justify their argument.

There are 90,000,000 people who speak Portuguese, because Portugal was the mother country of Brazil. English is the official language of British Honduras, Guyana, and a number of Caribbean Islands and has been adopted as a second language by millions of people throughout Latin America. French is the official language of Haiti. Chinese, Hindi, Arabic, and Slavic languages are also spoken by many new citizens. In addition there are countless native Indian languages spoken.

Customs. Because Latin America is a diverse blend of Indian, European, and African peoples, it is only logical that the customs of the people reflect those ingredients. Each culture has its unique characteristics. What is important and relevant to one group may not seem so to another. Persons interested in learning about Latin America must understand that customs must be seen as aspects of culture which grow, change, and become more varied as the society develops and industrializes. While customs or traits vary among the Latin American nations, there are a number that may be identified and associated with the greater culture.

Personalism. On a personal level, whether it be business or family relationships, Latin Americans value direct contact with the individual concerned. This is very likely a carry over from colonial rule when a colonist in a dispute with officials, at least in theory, could take an argument directly to the king.

Formalism. There appears to be an unwritten code in Latin America regarding the behavior of individuals. This may be seen in the manner and tense of verb used in speaking with strangers and family and friends. At a formal business meeting, for example, one always refers to the counterpart being addressed as *usted,* the formal word for "you." That same person speaking later in the day to his best friend, however, would use the less formal and familiar form, *tu.* Because of a high value placed on the worth of the individual, respect is given and is expected in return regardless of one's station in life. It is also the sign of respect and affection for men to embrace each other publicly in what is known as *un abrazo.*

Individualism. Another of the Spanish influences that remains strong among Latin Americans is the concept of the individual. In the best sense, it refers to the obligation that a person has to family, friends, and nation. Individuals recognize that they live in a framework of inter-dependency and adjust their behavior accordingly. Sometimes, however, a distortion of individualism takes place and the concept becomes radicalized. This kind of behavior which places an extreme emphasis on male pride, honor, and dominance is called *machismo.* In the most negative sense, *machismo* is displayed in the attitude of men toward women. The *macho* takes a domineering attitude in his relationships with women and regards them almost as objects instead of as persons.

Fatalism. This seems to be decreasing in importance as Latin America develops. It is a belief that events in life are inevitable and that one must often resign oneself to one's condition. An analysis of the Spanish language reveals that, unlike English, there is more use of the passive voice and the subjunctive mood suggesting that "things happen to you." A good example is seen in the simple phrase, "I dropped the dish." When the same thought is translated from the Spanish language, it says, "The dish dropped from my hands."

The Siesta. The *siesta* is a pleasant custom of napping or just relaxing after the noonday meal, which is the heaviest meal of the day. Banks, stores and places of business close from noon until 2 or 3 o'clock in many cities, but stay open until 7. In this relaxed atmosphere punctuality is less important than it is with North Americans.

Education. Education in Latin America differs in many respects from that in the United States. Only about half of the children ever attend school. The school year is from March to November because the seasons are reversed in most of South America. When it is summer in the United States, it is winter in Latin America. In most countries, school is held six days a week from 7:00 a.m. to 12 noon.

Control of education is usually vested in a government agency generally called the ministry of public education. The head of the ministry is appointed by the chief executive and is expected to carry out all educational laws. A large central office staff with many inspectors carries out the duties of the ministry. Every phase of education including curriculum development, administration, teacher certification, salary determination, and educational planning is controlled by the ministry. Periodically, schools are inspected by the central office. Thus, in Latin America, the responsibilities which the people in the United States delegate to their local school boards, school districts and state education departments, are centered in the ministry. Both public and private schools must meet the requirements set down by the ministry because pupils must prepare for official examinations.

Many Latin American countries have a 12-year school program as we do in the United States but others are based on an 11-year system. In some areas, pre-kindergartens and kindergartens are on the increase. Primary instruction usually lasts six years, but only about 20 percent of the children complete their primary education. Secondary schools known as *gimnasios, liceos* or *colegios nationales,* usually have a six-year program and prepare students for professional schools and colleges. Few courses, such as typing, home economics, or woodworking, which we have in the United States, are offered. Graduates of secondary schools are admitted without entrance examination to the universities for four- to seven-year courses. There are also specialized schools, run by the state, for agriculture, manual arts, commerce, music and art.

Secondary education is somewhat limited because Latin America does not have enough trained teachers. Many children have to help support their families by working in the fields. Often professional people, such as doctors and lawyers, devote a few hours a week to teaching. Much of the secondary education is still run by private church schools. Education is also difficult in regions where teachers often do not know the native languages, and natives cannot speak Spanish or Portuguese. In some areas, books and other reading materials are practically nonexistent.

As a result, the level of educational achievement varies widely from country to country—ranging from a literacy rate of about 90 percent in Argentina, Chile, Uruguay, and Costa Rica, to less than 50 percent in Bolivia and El Salvador. The record of Haiti is a dismal 20 percent.

Educating the Indians, especially those in remote areas, is a big problem to Latin America. The Indians, who maintain tribal connections, very often do not feel the need for formal schooling. The village may be the center of their lives. Many take little part in the political life of their nation.

Several countries, among them Brazil and Mexico, realize that the Indians cannot be active citizens in a modern industrial nation unless they are taught to read and write. As a result, a conscious effort has been made to close the gap between the coastal cities and the mountainous regions through programs of Indian education.

Mexico's program is typical. Teachers receive special training for their work before they go out into the villages. Each man or woman who is taught to read and write promises to teach someone else. At first the Indian language native to the village must be used, but later, especially with children, the change is made to Spanish. The ability to read and write Spanish lifts the Indians out of their limited environment. A national instead of a local language gives them an interest in the progress of the nation as a whole.

C. RELIGION AND INFLUENCE OF THE CHURCH

Roman Catholicism, the religion of Spain and Portugal, was carried to America by the friars who accompanied the *conquistadores* in their journey across the Atlantic Ocean. To the Spanish in particular, the Catholic religion was a matter of profound importance. They wanted to share it with the peoples of the New World. Spain had been previously conquered and ruled by the forces of Islam and it was the Catholic faith that symbolized resistance to the occupation. In the 15th century Catholicism served as the successful force for unification of the Christian armies that drove out the Muslims.

The Catholic missionaries worked intensively among the Indians. By the end of the 16th century, numerous converts had been made. In addition, the Church fathers championed the cause of the Indians when colonial administrators sought to exploit them.

With their primary mission accomplished, the Church began to amass great wealth over the years. The money came from sources such as *tithes* and inheritances. Gradually, the Church grew more conservative. Following independence, the Church tended to support the policies of the oligarchy. It often preached a doctrine which stressed the acceptance of the rigors of life for large numbers of the population. Liberal elements resented the privileged position of the Church and debated ways to reduce its status.

Over the past several decades, however, the Church has moved away from its conservative position and has been in the forefront in the quest for greater social justice in Latin America.

Since the Vatican II meeting of the bishops of the Church in Rome in the early 1960's, a new effort has been made to rethink the role of the Church in its relations with the people and the state. This was interpreted by some as an invitation to bring the Church into a greater social role and, hence, in conflict with established order. By the time of the Latin American Bishops Conference at Medellin, Colombia, in 1968, a new attitude toward the poor was formed. No longer was poverty looked upon as something to be accepted with resignation or humility. Instead, it was seen by the Church as a condition caused and carried on by the power structures in the society. In 1979, another bishops' meeting was held in Puebla, Mexico. Pope John Paul II spoke at this meeting and urged that priests avoid becoming too involved in social and political issues. However, he did affirm the defense of human rights, the links between the gospel and human promotion, and the rights of workers and peasants to organize to better their economic position. Today, the Church in Latin America is acknowledged as the chief protector of human rights and the only institution to serve as a check upon the excesses of the state.

The Influence of Other Religions. Not only has the Catholic Church modified its position in Latin America over the years, but Protestant evangelism has also had an influence upon large numbers of people. This religion first came to Latin America when masses of immigrants from Europe arrived in the 19th century. Liberal leaders who were not happy about the power of the Catholic Church encouraged the establishment of Protestant missions. The large expanses of territory and the lack of Catholic priests to minister to the needs of the faithful has created a vacuum which the Protestant churches have filled with great success.

Jews fleeing persecution in Europe found havens in Latin America and practice their faith freely there. Latin America remains a predominantly Catholic culture however. Today, the actual practice of the faith centers not so much upon church attendance (where figures are low), but around the traditional religious ceremonies relating to birth, marriage, and death with a strong belief in personal moral convictions.

Patron Saints. It is the traditional practice of the family to name each child after a particular saint, religious object, or religious event. Names such as Rosario (rosary) or Asunción (Ascension) are not uncommon. Travelers to Latin American countries will notice calendars placed in the windows of many shops and stores. These calendars remind people of the day set aside each year to honor saints. In Latin America, one's birthday is secondary in importance to the observance and celebration of the saint whose name is given to the child.

In addition, many cities and towns have their own patron saint whose day is also frequently marked by celebrations and fiestas. These fiestas provide an opportunity for communal participation, and release from the everyday life of routines. In effect, they are an important social act.

Hamilton Wright

Christ of the Andes symbolizes peace between Argentina and Chile. The inscription reads: "Sooner shall these mountains crumble into dust than the peoples of Argentina and Chile break the peace which at the feet of Christ, the Redeemer, they have sworn to maintain."

D. LITERATURE, ART, AND ARCHITECTURE

Literature. The first authors of Spanish colonial literature were the explorers and *conquistadores* who wrote of their experiences. They produced a literature about heroes, wars, Indian civilizations, and the New World. The first writer about America was Christopher Columbus (1451–1506) with his *Letter on the Discovery (Carta sobre el descubrimiento)* and his *Journal (Diario)*. Cortés (1485-1547) wrote from Mexico to Charles V, King of Spain. His famous five letters, *Cartas de relación,* described the civilization and conquest of the Aztecs of Mexico. Bartolomé de las Casas (1474-1566), a Spanish priest, denounced the terrible treatment Indians received from their conquerors. His chronicle, *General History of the Indies (Historia general de las Indias)*, also asked for better treatment of the natives. The conquest of Mexico was also recorded by Bernal Diaz del Castillo (1496–1584) in his *True History of the New Spain (Historia verdadera de la Conquista de le Nueva España)*. The first great writer to be born in Latin America was Garcilaso de la Vega (1539–1616), known as "el Inca." He was the author of *The Royal Commentaries (Los Comentarios reales)* which included a history of the Incas and an account of the civil wars in Peru.

One of the great poems in the Spanish language is "La Arancaña," which praises the bravery and courage of the Indians of Chile in their wars with the Spanish. It was written by Alonso de Ercilla y Zúñiga, a captain in the Spanish army.

In the years following independence, intellectual life in Latin America was barely developed. The turbulence of instability and *caudillo* rule did little to encourage the arts and literature. The gulf between the educated elite and the masses (some 80 percent of whom were illiterate) meant a limited demand for cultural pursuits. The oligarchy saw little around them that stimulated intellectual interest. Instead, those who sought culture and intellectual thought looked to leadership from the Old World, and especially to France. Latin American writers imitated European styles and themes. Domingo Sarmiento (1811-1888), in his book *Civilization and Barbarism,* identified urban life with the localism of rural Argentina.

Perhaps the most important work to come out of Argentina in the same period was written by José Hernandez (1834-1886), and was titled *Martin Fierro.* The hero of this epic work was the Argentine *gaucho,* symbol of the bold reality of life on the pampa. In the later part of the 19th century, there developed in Latin America a new artistic movement. It marked a radical departure from previous artistic and literary expression and was reflected in contemporary works. The movement was called Modernism.

The Modernists, led by such writers as Ruben Dario (1867-1916), denounced materialism and championed non-personal values. José Marti (1853-1895) took issue with Sarmiento and argued against dividing Latin America into the "civilized and the barbarians." In *Our America,* he said that the barbarians had qualities that would finally prove more valuable than those copied from the Old World.

By the first quarter of the 20th century the intellectuals of Latin America were undergoing a change in their thinking. The emergence of the United States as a major world power following its victory over the Spanish in 1898 was a major source of discomfort throughout the region. The best expression of this fear, resentment, and jealousy over the powerful Yankee neighbor to the north was José Rodo's (1871-1917) *Ariel.* North Americans, according to Rodo, were successful, but their success was hollow because of their materialism and lack of culture. Latin America, by contrast, was superior to Yankee culture because of the spirituality of its people.

Artists and writers were also forced to re-examine their attitudes when Europe became involved in a brutal war in 1914. Previously, this region of the world had been viewed as the "seat" of culture. Perhaps, it was reasoned, Latin Americans should look elsewhere for their models.

Beginning in the 1920s, Latin American writers and poets

began to focus upon themes in their regions and countries. The literature reveals the identification of the writer with the social ills of poverty, illiteracy, and exploitation, both domestic and foreign. In this period the writer, more than any other individual, becomes the conscience of society.

Today, the most important group of novelists lives in northeastern Brazil. They are called the regionalist writers. They write about life in the cities, life on plantations, factory workers, schools, juvenile delinquency, and all kinds of social problems. Important among these writers are José Lins do Rego, Amenco de Almerda, and the "novelist of Rio," Marques Rebélo.

The modern Latin American literary movement has been marked by the growth of publishing houses in such cities as Buenos Aires, Rio de Janeiro, Sao Paulo, and Mexico City. Latin America was honored, in 1945, with the awarding of the Nobel Prize for literature to Gabriela Mistral, the Chilean poet. Miguel Angel Asturias of Guatemala received this prize in 1967, and it was awarded to Pablo Neruda of Chile in 1971.

"Mother Earth," a painting by Diego Rivera, depicts the cycle of life, from seed to flower, from mother to child.

Art and Architecture. Art played an important role in the Latin American revolutions for independence. The walls of public buildings were used to explain the countries' histories. Even the most illiterate peasant could understand a picture.

World famous Mexican painters include Diego Rivera (1886–1957), who merged Indian designs with bright colors to create a modern effect, and José Clemente Orozco (1883–1949), who applied dazzling color to frescoes in starkly simple style. They have painted in the murals of public buildings the story of the Indian race and its enslavement by the Spaniards. David Alfaro Siqueiros, another Mexican, has painted numerous works which depict the problems and struggles of the worker.

Some of the greatest painters of the 20th century are Indians or *mestizos. Mestizo* art has something new to say to the world because it draws its strength from the same sources that built the magnificent temples and splendid palaces of ancient Indian races.

These details of Juan O'Gorman's "Independence Mural" show several aspects of the Mexican struggle for national freedom.

A modern sculpture of *"Justizia"* (Justice) seated in front of the Supreme Court building in Brazil's new capital city, Brasília.

Brazil is noted for its religious art, which dates back practically to the country's discovery four and a half centuries ago. Along with the Portuguese colonizers came the priests of the *"Companhia de Jesus,"* the Jesuit order of the Catholic Church. In the older cities it is not unusual to find churches more than 300 years old. In Salvador, Brazil, it is said there are 365 churches; one for each day of the year.

In recent years, Brazil has taken full advantage of a generation of architects to make its public buildings the envy of the world. Oscar Niemeyer is famous as the designer and principal architect of the new capital city of Brasília. Alfonso Eduardo Reidy designed the Brazilian Museum of Modern Art.

E. THE HOME AND FAMILY

In Latin America the home is the center of most social activities. Birthdays, weddings, and saints' days are all occasions for family get-togethers and celebrations. Strangers are welcomed with the greeting, *"Mi casa es su casa,"* meaning "My house is your house."

The Family. In the traditional Latin American home, the father is the head of the household, and each family member has a clearly defined function. The Latin American family unit is usually an extended family. Households often consist of grandparents, parents, and children. In addition, other relatives very often live nearby and there is a wide sharing of social experiences among them. The interests of the family come first, and cooperation and assistance is provided for those members who face economic difficulty.

Among the more unique patterns of social life is the concept of godparenthood. Generally, there is a special relationship between a child's godparents (*padrinos*) and his parents (*padres*). The use of the term *compadre* conveys this closeness. The *padrino,* who is loved, respected, and honored, and recognized as a "family member," assumes the role upon the child's baptism. In the event of death of the child's parents, the godparents assume the responsibility of raising the godchild (*ahijado*).

Marriage. Dating customs of most Latin Americans are still quite strict. The boy not only needs the girl's permission to visit her but her parents' permission as well.

The young people are usually chaperoned when they leave the house, and the girl's family is always present while they are at home. In some of the larger liberal metropolitan cities today, young couples may go to large parties unchaperoned. However, they never single or double date alone. When a couple decides to get married, either the young man's parents, relatives, godparents or all of them, ask the girl's parents for their permission.

Several visits are required because the girl's parents want to make sure she is getting a good husband. They also do not want to give the impression that they are anxious for their daughter to be married.

The wedding ceremony takes place in church, usually after elaborate preparations. Rich and poor alike present their best appearance at this ceremony which is followed by a celebration with food, drink, and dancing.

A Latin American girl does not give up her last (family) name when she marries. If Maria Zilembo marries José de Paso, she becomes Maria Zilembo de Paso. Her son, Juan, would be known as Juan de Paso Zilembo. All children bear a given name, the father's family (last) name and the mother's family (last) name, in that sequence.

The Domestic Scene. The rural Latin American house has undergone little change over the years; it is still made of logs or sun-dried bricks of earth or clay. Its roof is covered with any available material—leaves, grass, or branches.

Traditionally, the rich have lived in the cities and the poor in the countryside. The city house is designed after those in Spain. Stone walls, which are painted white, are used to keep out the heat, but most rooms open onto a patio which is the center of family activity because it is cool. The patio helps to insure the maximum circulation of air, which is important in a region which is usually very hot.

Although foods vary from country to country in Latin America, tomatoes, potatoes, corn (maize), avocados, and cocoa are common to all countries. Mangoes, breadfruit and papayas are favorite fruits. Each country has its own favorite dishes. In Argentina, which produces fine beef cattle, it is *ossobuco.* This beef stew is made with tomato paste and wine and served with cabbage which has been cooked with the meat. Bolivia is famous for its *empanaditas de quesso* or cheese turnovers.

The national dish of Brazil is *feijoada,* black beans cooked with sausage, beef, and bacon. *Pollo ranchero,* baked chicken

73

cooked with white wine and onions, is popular in Mexico. *Llapingachos,* a dish enjoyed in Ecuador, consists of potatoes stuffed with cream cheese and eggs and served with a sauce made of onions and tomatoes. *Torta de queso* or cheese cake is famous in Venezuela, while *yema quemada* or candied egg yolks are enjoyed in Uruguay. *Tarta de uvas chiffon* (grape chiffon pie) is eaten in Peru, while *postre de guineo* or banana pudding is a favorite dessert in Nicaragua.

Most Latin Americans dress conservatively. White trousers and shirts are worn by men in rural areas, and women wear white blouses and dark skirts. In great metropolitan areas, the people dress as North Americans do. Fashionable sports jackets and suits with white shirts and ties are worn by the men while the women wear the latest fashions from all over the world.

Garments of traditional design are still worn by Indians in Latin America. The *quexquemel,* worn in Mexico, is a long piece of cloth with an opening for the head; it is worn over the shoulders as a cape. Straw hats (*sombreros*) are worn by men everywhere in Latin America.

F. MUSIC, FUN AND DANCING

Dancing is very popular and is a major form of expression. Latin American dance has been influenced by Indian, Spanish, Portuguese, and African cultures all of which have contributed to its music and rhythm.

The Indians have their own traditional dances, and some still wear masks to represent animals or demons. The Spanish and Portuguese brought their own European dances with them, and these merged with the dances of the Indians. The combination resulted in the *mestizo* dance, complete with masks. The characteristic *zapateado* or heel-beating step has been incorporated into such national dances as the *cueca* of Chile, the *sanjuanito* of Ecuador, the *marinera* of Peru, and the *seis zapateo* of Puerto Rico.

The Latin American dances which are most familiar to Americans—the rhumba, samba, conga, mambo and cha-cha-cha—are mixtures of African rhythms and European melodies. Jazz music today is taking on an international beat. Although the *bossa nova* and *merengue* are still popular in some areas, in many urban metropolitan areas young people dance the skate, hustle, and the latest disco dances.

Composers who have won international fame include Heitor Villa-Lobos (Brazil), Juan José Castro (Argentina), Domingo Santa Cruz (Chile), Carlos Cháver (Mexico), and Amadeo Roldan (Cuba). Large cities, such as Buenos Aires, have some of the finest opera houses in the world.

Sports. There is no question that "futebol" is the most popular sport in Latin America. In the United States, futebol is called soccer. Soccer is more than a game in Latin America, it is almost a way of life. Each year contests are held pitting one country's best players against another. The rivalries between teams are so intense that the outcome results in a national celebration for the winner and close to a day of mourning for the loser. Soccer fans in Latin America take the sport so seriously that they have been known to physically assault team players and umpires for unsatisfactory performance or for unpopular decisions. In 1964, in Lima, in a soccer match between the Peruvian national team and the team from Argentina, a riot erupted when the referee reversed his decision on a Peruvian goal causing the game to be lost to the visitors. At the end of the day, 319 people had died and hundreds were injured victims of the riot over the decision.

In terms of playing ability, Latin Americans are regarded as excellent soccer players, and many of the stars of the North American Soccer League come from that region. Perhaps the greatest soccer player who ever lived is Pelé. Born Edson Arantes do Nascimento, Pelé comes from Brazil.

Many professional baseball players of North America play on Latin American teams in the off-season. Although bull-fighting is not universal in Latin America, as most people think, it can be found in Mexico, Panama, and Peru. Cockfighting is a popular spectator sport and is legal throughout the Caribbean. *Jai alai,* another spectator sport, is a game resembling handball, played by two or four players with a ball and a long, curved basket strapped to the wrist. Argentinians are famous the world over for their thoroughbred horses and horsemanship.

QUESTIONS AND ACTIVITIES

KEY WORDS, PEOPLE, AND PHRASES

Can you define or identify the following words or names? Use an encyclopedia, if necessary.

Old World	individualism	exploit	status
quadroons	convert	oligarchy	*padrino*
mulattoes	missionaries	doctrine	futebol
castellano	*siesta*	liberal	*gimnasios*
La Raza Cosmica	*un abrazo*	pampa	Pelé

MULTIPLE CHOICE TEST

In the following you have four possible choices. Select the only correct answer.

1. The children of a European-Indian marriage are called *(a) mestizos, (b)* Indians, *(c) criollos, (d)* Negroes.
2. Which of the following make up most of the total population of South America? *(a) mestizos, (b)* Spaniards, *(c) criollos, (d)* Negroes.
3. Murals, art on the walls of public buildings, have been an important kind of painting in Latin America. The world-famous Mexican painter who merged Indian designs with bright colors to create a modern effect in his murals was *(a)* Pablo Neruda, *(b)* Heitor Villa-Lobos, *(c)* Diego Rivera, *(d)* Oscar Niemeyer.
4. Which term best describes a typical Latin American's attitude toward strangers? *(a)* hostile, *(b)* cool, *(c)* suspicious, *(d)* friendly.
5. The symbol of authority in a Latin American family is the *(a)* oldest son, *(b)* mother, *(c)* father, *(d)* oldest daughter.

6. The main reason for the Spanish arrival in the New World was the search for *(a)* religion, *(b)* adventure, *(c)* riches, *(d)* freedom.
7. People in Latin America who speak Spanish call their language *(a)* español, *(b)* castellano, *(c)* lingua mexico, *(d)* el idioma.
8. Control of education in Latin America is vested in the *(a)* ministry of public education, *(b)* board of education, *(c)* state board of regents, *(d)* mayor of the town.
9. Latin American writers who denounced trends in life toward materialism were known as *(a)* Modernists, *(b)* Radicals, *(c)* Conservatives, *(d)* Reactionaries.
10. An aspect of religion found in Latin America which is not found in the United States is *(a)* missionary activity, *(b)* a state religion, *(c)* church schools, *(d)* church social functions.
11. The first authors of Spanish colonial literature wrote about *(a)* romance, *(b)* mystery, *(c)* wars, *(d)* humor.
12. The 16th-century priest who denounced Indian mistreatment was *(a)* Sarmiento, *(b)* de las Casas, *(c)* del Castillo, *(d)* de la Vega.
13. *Martin Fierro,* the story of the *gaucho,* was written by *(a)* Sarmiento, *(b)* Hernandez, *(c)* Dario, *(d)* Rodo.
14. Where have the rich and poor traditionally lived in Latin America? *(a)* The rich have lived in the countryside and the poor in the cities. *(b)* The poor have lived in the countryside and the rich in the cities. *(c)* Both rich and poor live in the countryside. *(d)* Both rich and poor live in the cities.
15. The most popular sport in Latin America is *(a)* baseball, *(b)* basketball, *(c)* soccer, *(d)* fishing.

THINGS TO DO

1. Prepare a report on the famous Mexican murals painted by 20th-century artists. Concentrate on the works of one specific artist. Discuss the major themes of these murals and why they have become such an important form of art.
2. Prepare an essay entitled "If." *(a)* "If people from the United States had settled Latin America," *(b)* "If everyone in Latin America could read and write."
3. Research project: Trace the influence that Spain had on the social organization of Latin America.
4. Prepare an "eye-witness" television description of a *(a)* bull-fight, *(b)* fiesta.

5. Interview a person from Latin America and write a report on dating and chaperones.
6. Present an oral report describing what you think is the most outstanding Latin American contribution to world culture.
7. Ask your home economics teacher to help you prepare some Latin American food for your class such as *feijoada* or *ossobuco*.
8. Prepare a report on Latin American folk songs or popular music. What are important themes?

5

MEXICO: GATEWAY TO LATIN AMERICA

A. THE LAND

Mexico, the only Latin American country to share a border with the United States, is the third largest of our southern neighbors. Its boundaries stretch for 8,300 miles around an area of almost 761,000 square miles. California, Arizona, and New Mexico border it on the northwest, and the Rio Grande River flows for over 1,000 miles to separate Mexico from Texas. The Gulf of Mexico is on the east, Guatemala and Belize on the south, and the Pacific Ocean is on the west. The Baja California Peninsula stretches 760 miles southward from American California on the west and is separated from the mainland by the Gulf of California. The Yucatán Peninsula on the east is a flat jungle-like area that is barely above sea level.

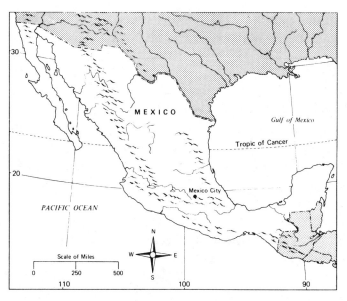

TOPOGRAPHICAL MAP OF MEXICO

Much of Mexico is mountainous with narrow, hot coastal plains. The high central plateau is flanked on the east by the Sierra Madre Oriental range which parallels the coast of the Gulf of Mexico. On the west, the Sierra Madre Occidental runs parallel to the Pacific coast. The Sierra Madre del Sur joins the two long coastal ranges and has many lofty volcanoes, the most famous of which is Popocatepetl.

Although Mexico lies mostly in the tropical zone, it has hot, temperate, and cool areas. The climate varies with the altitude. There is a dry season from November to May and a rainy season from June to October. The southern coasts have hot, humid weather (*tierras calientas*); the plateau regions have a temperate climate (*tierras templades*); and the mountain areas have cold weather *(tierras frias)*.

Mexico City, the capital, is the oldest city on the North American continent. It is located in central Mexico at an altitude of 7,800 feet above sea level. Its climate is cool and dry. Other important cities located on the central plateau are Guadalajara, Monterrey, and Puebla. Acapulco and Mazatlán are harbors on the Pacific; Tampico and Vera Cruz are important ports on the Gulf of Mexico.

B. HISTORY

Pre-Columbian Mexico had been inhabited by many Indian tribes. The three most noted for their highly developed civilizations were the Mayas, Toltecs, and Aztecs. Each civilization contributed much to the culture and art of Mexico.

The Mayas, who have been called the "Greeks of the New World" entered the Yucatán Peninsula in the sixth century. They were the builders of Chichén-Itzá, Mayapán, and Uxmal. The pyramids and temples of Tenayuca Tula, Teotihuacán, and Xochicalo were built by the Toltecs, who disappeared from the area after about 400 years. For a few centuries the Valley of Mexico or Anahuac was inhabited by other tribes, most important of which were the Aztecs.

The Aztecs were a northern tribe who moved south because of the poor climate and bad soil in the area where they were living. They wandered for more than a century since they were not welcomed by the tribes already in the area. When they entered the Valley of Mexico it was a land of lakes dotted by small islands. On an island in Lake Texcoco they built their capital and called it Tenochtitlán in 1325, the beginning of Mexican history. Within a century the city became the richest and most famous of all of Latin America.

The Spaniards Arrive. The first Spaniards to reach Mexico were shipwrecked sailors who landed on the coast of Yucatán in 1512. However, Francisco Hernández de Cordoba, who landed on the peninsula in 1517, is credited with discovering Mexico. In 1518 the area was named "New Spain" by Juan de Grijalva. The Spanish governor of Cuba sent Hernán Cortés in 1519 to see if the reports reaching him about Mexico's abundance of gold were really true.

Cortés sailed into Vera Cruz harbor when the Aztec Empire was at its height. Its ruler, Montezuma II, believing the Spaniards to be the invincible army of the god-king Quetzalcoatl, sent envoys to greet them bearing gifts of gold and silver. This only whetted the appetite of Cortés for more gold and more silver. He marched on the fabled capital city of Tenochtitlán. Though he was greeted by Montezuma as a friend, he and his men set out to conquer the Aztecs. By 1521 Tenochtitlán and all of Mexico fell to Cortés and Spain.

The Spaniards began a rule that lasted for 300 years. Almost immediately they rebuilt the capital which they renamed Mexico City. They used the stones of the existing Aztec temples for building Christian churches, schools, and other buildings. The first governor was Antonio de Mendoza who wisely and capably established orderly government and schools, and tried to help the Indians develop mining and agriculture.

However, during the years following the rule of Mendoza, the Spaniards introduced their colonial system of high taxes, restrictions and abuse, the result of which was a growing feeling of nationalism and unrest. Dissatisfaction with the political power of the Church and with the Spanish mercantilist system, which drained Mexico of its mineral wealth, stirred the people to active rebellion.

The Fight for Independence.   A country priest named Miguel Hidalgo y Costilla issued the famous *"grito de Dolores"* ("down with bad government, death to the Spaniards") and rallied a poorly clad army against Spain in 1811. His army met with several successes in the fight for freedom, but when he turned away from the capital, Mexico City, Hidalgo lost the initiative and was captured and slain by the Spaniards.

The desire for independence did not die with Hidalgo. The fight was carried on by another priest, Father José Maria Morelos, an outstanding soldier and organizer. He was able to gain control over the southern half of Mexico, and proclaimed independence at the Congress of Chilpango before his capture and execution in 1815. For several years guerrilla warfare was waged against the Spaniards. In 1821 General Augustín de Iturbide captured Mexico City and established a short-lived empire.

The Birth of the Republic.   In 1822 General Antonio Lopez de Santa Anna declared Mexico a republic. In 1824 the Mexican Congress adopted a constitution which called for a "federal, popular republic." Slaves were freed, titles of nobility were abolished and other steps were taken to develop a democratic society. A period of strife among leaders brought a series of presidents for the next several decades.

General Santa Anna ruled Mexico and its politics from 1833 to 1855, first as military leader, then as president, then as dictator. He led Mexico into war twice with the United States—in 1836 when Texas declared its independence from Spain, and again in 1846 when Mexico lost all its territory from the Rio Grande to Oregon. Two years after Santa Anna's resignation in 1855, a new constitution was adopted providing for a more liberal and democratic government.

Benito Juárez was President of Mexico from 1858 to 1872. During his presidency, civil war erupted between the supporters of the constitution and the land-owners, backed by the priests. The forces of Juárez put down the revolution, and during the following period of reconstruction Napoleon III sent Archduke Maximilian of Austria to rule Mexico as emperor. Maximilian's army forced Juárez into exile, but he carried on guerrilla warfare until 1867 when Maximilian was captured and executed. Juárez then governed until 1872.

In 1877 Porfirio Díaz was elected president and remained in power as a dictator until 1910 when a revolution broke out. During the Díaz rule, Mexico saw a period of peace and prosperity marked by material development and increased foreign investments, but there were still serious unsolved social and economic problems. Living conditions for the majority of the people were terrible. Education stagnated, and roads were in frightful condition. Francisco Madero led the revolutionaries against Díaz, who resigned in 1911. Madero, however, could not stabilize the government, and was subsequently assassinated.

The revolutionary forces split up and were reassembled in different parts of Mexico. Venustiano Carranza became known as the Constitutionalist; Pancho Villa was the outlaw and revolutionary; and Emiliano Zapata was the leader for agrarian reforms. In 1917, Carranza emerged the victor. His government set forth a new constitution calling for universal suffrage, labor reforms, freedom of religion, division of large estates, confiscation of church property, and government ownership of national resources. The constitution, with its amendments, is still in force today.

A semblance of peace returned to Mexico with the election of General Alvaro Obregón in 1920, who encouraged the organization of unions. However, Obregón had many political difficulties and even went so far as to expel the Vatican's apostolic delegate.

He was succeeded in 1924 by Plutarco Elías Calles, who dominated the government for ten years. His policy toward the Church caused open warfare; he closed churches and deported priests. For three years priests did not say mass in their churches. But in 1929 a settlement was reached with the Church.

Obregón was reelected in 1928 but was assassinated by a religious fanatic, thereby leaving Calles in control for the next six years. While not actually the president, he named and dominated those who held office.

General Lázaro Cárdenas was elected president in 1934. He instituted a six-year plan for social, economic, and educational reforms and increased the number of collective land projects known as *ejidos* (lands held and cultivated by Indians). Cárdenas built irrigation projects and power plants. He hoped to unify the country by building railroads and highways. In 1938 Cárdenas nationalized the Mexican oil fields.

During the presidency of Manuel Avila Camacho (1940–1946) Mexico joined with the United States in declaring war against the Axis powers in World War II. In 1945 a 300-man squadron from Mexico was sent to the front lines in the Philippines. During Camacho's term the Social Security Institute was founded and education reforms were instituted.

Miguel Alemán, the next president of Mexico, sought to further agricultural development and industrialization. However, his presidency was noted for the *mordida* (graft) and corruption.

In 1952 Adolfo Ruiz Cortines was elected president and continued the policies of Camacho and Alemán. During the presidency of Adolfo López Mateos in 1958, street riots erupted in Mexico City over a bus-fare increase. A nationwide strike of railroad workers was called in an effort to rid the labor unions of government domination.

Gustavo Díaz Ordaz, was elected in 1964 and served until 1970. He instituted a five-year plan for domestic development supported by private enterprise. On October 28, 1967, Mexico signed a treaty with the United States which settled a century-old border dispute. Under the terms of the treaty, the United States ceded to Mexico the territory known as El Chamizal, 437 acres of land lost by Mexico when the Rio Grande changed its course in 1864.

While some Mexicans learn industrial skills in an automobile plant in Mexico City, others work as potters using the skills developed by their ancestors.

In 1970, Luis Echeverría Alvarez was elected president. Despite his promise to finish the "unfinished business of the 1910 revolution," Echeverría's presidency was marked by a number of disturbances and student riots. People accused the president of being responsible for the massacre of a number of university students in 1968, when he was Minister of the Interior. Echeverría's administration is best remembered for his attempts to direct Mexico to a position of leadership among the developing nations. Chief among his goals was to change the economic relations between the Third World and the developed nations, especially the United States. However, Mexico's economy faltered during the Echeverría years. In his last year in office, 1976, he had to devalue the *peso,* the national currency, some 39 percent.

In 1976, José Lopez Portillo was sworn in as president of the Mexican republic. Confident of Mexico's new potential as a world leader because of its vast petroleum reserves, Portillo has taken a cautious approach in his international dealings. Fearful of runaway inflation if too much foreign exchange enters Mexico in return for oil, he has kept controls on production.

C. THE GOVERNMENT AND THE CONSTITUTION

The Constitution of 1917 declared Mexico a federal republic composed of 29 states, two territories, and the Federal District. All those powers not granted to the federal government are reserved to the states; but the states' powers are not nearly as extensive as those in the United States.

Executive power is vested in the president who is elected by direct popular vote for a six-year term. He cannot succeed himself. The president proposes and executes the laws of Congress; he legislates by executive decree in certain economic and financial areas. There is no vice-president, so if the president is disabled or dies during the first three years of his term, the Congress elects a provisional president and calls for a national election to name a new president. If the president is unable to serve during the latter part of his term in office, the new president is elected directly by the Congress. There is no system of checks and balances on the president because he controls the legislative and judicial branches of government. The president has the power to overrule any decision made by Congress and can force the resignation of those who oppose him.

The Mexican Congress consists of a Senate and Chamber of Deputies. There are 60 senators, two from each state and the Federal District, all of whom are elected by direct vote for a six-year term. The Chamber of Deputies has 210 members, elected by direct vote for three-year terms. Each state has at least two deputies and each territory a minimum of one. Senators and deputies may not succeed themselves. The Congress has the power to legislate on all matters concerning the national government.

The judicial arm of the government is composed of a Supreme Court, circuit, and district courts. The 21 Supreme Court judges are appointed by the president with senatorial approval. Local and federal judges are appointed by the Supreme Court.

Political Parties.   The Institutional Revolutionary Party (*Partido Revolucionario Institutional*—PRI) has been the controlling political force in Mexico since 1929. It has been powerful enough to elect all the presidential, congressional, and state candidates since that time. The PRI is not really a political party but a means for providing support for the government through political campaigns, organizing political demonstrations, and providing jobs to ambitious bureaucrats willing to work within the party system.

Foreign Relations.   Mexico, because of its location, size, population, and wealth in petroleum, seeks a louder voice in world affairs. Because of its historical relations with the United States, Mexico has tried to maintain a position of independence in hemispheric affairs. This is true even when that independence places Mexico in conflict with United States policy goals. For example, Mexico has consistently refused to support measures to give more strength to the peacekeeping machinery of the Organization of American States. Mexico fears that the United States will utilize that body to intervene in hemispheric affairs. In the future, Mexico can be expected to further assert its independence as a leader of the Latin American nations.

D. THE PEOPLE AND CULTURE

Mexico's over 67,000,000 people are Indian, Spanish, and *mestizo*. Approximately 15 percent are pure Indian. They live in isolated areas and speak their own languages rather than Spanish—the language of the land. Another 10 percent of the people have European backgrounds. The great 75 percent of the population is *mestizo*—Indian and Spanish. Most Mexicans belong to the Roman Catholic Church.

The culture of Mexico is a fusion of Amerindian, Spanish, and Catholic; the Indian heritage of the Mayas and the Aztecs is reflected in all areas of Mexican life. The Mayas were farming people, but they were also great artists, architects, and mathematicians. The Aztecs were experts at governing and organizing. Their religion was complex. Mexico derives its name from the Aztec god, Mexitli.

This mixture of Indian and Spanish culture has produced a people who are, by nature, courteous and friendly. They look forward to great social, economic, and cultural improvement with a strong sense of nationalism.

Customs. Mexicans take a mid-day nap, called a *siesta*. Families celebrate the pilgrimage to Bethlehem for nine days before Christmas. Each evening ends with the breaking of the *piñata* by a blindfolded child. The gaily decorated package, suspended from the ceiling, spills out small gifts, candies, and coins.

The Mexicans celebrate the beginning of their independence movement on September 16, commemorating Father Hidalgo's announcement of the beginning of the revolution.

Mexico, too, has its Carnival, a pre-Lenten party. There is always a *fiesta* somewhere since each city, town and village has a patron saint who must be venerated.

Education. Mexican education began under the auspices of the Roman Catholic Church. The Franciscan Order started schools to educate the Indians. In 1551 the first North American college, the Royal and Pontifical University of Mexico, was founded.

Today the public school system includes kindergarten through the secondary grades. Education is free and compulsory for all children between the ages of six and 15. Mexico's literacy rate is now over 75 percent. Through education, the government is making a great effort to assimilate the Indians into the mainstream of national life.

The Arts. Spaniards began building churches in Mexico as soon as they settled the land. The ever-increasing tempo of church building continued until a dozen new churches were being opened each month. At first these churches were dark gloomy fortress-like structures which were inspired by Gothic influences. But as the Spanish became wealthier they thanked the Lord for their affluence by building extravagant churches. José de Churriguera, the architect of the great cathedral in Salamanca, Spain, became the source of inspiration for Mexican church design. One of the most striking examples of baroque curves and the twisted geometric columns of Mexican Churrigueresque is found in the architecture and altar pieces of the Ocotlan Sanctuary.

Modern architecture has been popular since the 1930's and has taken various forms. The use of glass facades and structures on stilts makes one think of the buildings in Chicago and New York. The difference, however, is the Mexicans' striking use of color. Excellent examples of modern architecture may be found in the Colonial Arcades, Tlacotalpan, Satellite City, and the Three Cultures Plaza in Mexico City.

Religion dominated architecture and the entire spectrum of the arts. Sculpture was created not only in stone but also in wood, with astoundingly realistic results. The Mexican Indians were traditionally adept at working with gold and silver.

Mexico is called the "land of handicrafts." Typical items for which the country is famous are textiles, including colorful *serapes,* tooled leather, glassware, and carvings.

Some good academic painting was produced during the 19th century and noteworthy Mexican artists made contributions in

CASE INQUIRY: Mexican Independence

Holidays often tell quite a lot about a people's history and way of life.

> On the night of the fifteenth of September in the year 1810 Father Miguel Hidalgo y Costilla stood on the balcony of the town hall in Dolores, Guanajuato, and called upon the townfolks to rise up against the Spanish government. Early the following morning, the Independence Revolution was launched. In 1822—a year after independence had been won—September 16 was established as National Independence Day and a custom inaugurated which has been repeated every year . . .
>
> Each year at 11:00 p.m. on the night of the fifteenth, Hidalgo's call to arms, known as the Grito de Dolores, is re-enacted in every city and town of Mexico. In the capital, it is the president himself who gives the thrilling cry from the balcony of the National Palace. The crowds below in the *zócalo* (main square) echo the *grito* as the president rings the liberty bell which is said to be the one used by Padre Hidalgo. Immediately all of the great bells of the Metropolitan Cathedral, which flanks the *zócalo* on the north side, burst into a deafening clamor; factory whistles, automobile horns, and a wide variety of noisemakers add to the din. In the state capitals the governors do the honors, and in other cities, towns, and villages the municipal president officiates. Everywhere the *grito* is followed by fireworks and general merrymaking. . . .
>
> On the sixteenth there are military parades in the larger cities and parades of school children in the smaller places. . . . In San Miguel de Allende the independence holidays become a full-fledged production which lasts for about two weeks. There are parades of elaborate floats with historical tableaux, [scenes] rodeos, bullfights, fireworks, and both native and popular dances.

1. What does the festival of September 16 celebrate? Does the holiday have an American counterpart? How does such a holiday help weld a nation's people together?

2. What can you learn from this holiday about Mexican life and history? About the Mexican temperament?

Fiesta Time in Latin America by Jean Milne. The Ward Ritchie Press, Los Angeles, 1965, pages 145–146.

the fields of landscape, portrait and religious art. José Guadalupe Posada was a forerunner of the modern muralists.

Mural painting may be Mexico's greatest contribution to the world's art. It is the most influential movement in the plastic arts in the Western Hemisphere today. In Mexico this form of art is supported and directed by the government. Three of the world's outstanding masters of the mural art are Diego Rivera, José Clemente Orozco, and David Alfaro Siqueriros. Their works appear in numerous public buildings and have been acclaimed throughout the world. Rufino Tamayo has painted both in Mexico and the United States and has expressed Mexican art in terms of universal values, overlooking political content.

Labor. Mexico's first labor law was enacted in 1936. There is no distinction between laborer and office worker. A maximum eight-hour working day and a weekly day of rest are guaranteed to everyone by the constitution. Night work is limited to seven hours with double pay for overtime. There are minimum wage and workmen's compensation laws. Labor is guaranteed the right to organize unions, and management has the right to form associations to protect its interests. More than 80 percent of the industrial force of Mexico shares in management's profits.

The first national labor union, the Regional Confederation of Mexican Workers, was organized in 1918. This combination of industrial and craft workers is the leading union in Mexico and has a great deal of power.

The first Social Security Law was passed in 1942 and set up the Mexican Social Security Institute which guarantees medical and financial assistance to workers. Government employees have other social security benefits.

Housing. A population boom in the cities has increased the shortage of housing. Mexico's Immediate Action Plans seek to combat this shortage by building an estimated 42,000 housing units yearly for an extended period of time. An interesting aspect of this program is that employers and labor union members are permitted to finance jointly the building of cooperative

One of Mexico's greatest challenges in the next decade is providing the food, housing, and jobs for a rapidly growing population. The mother in this picture is only 15 years old.

Daniel J. Mugan

housing projects. The Banco de Mexico, with the help of the federal government, has extended credit, loans, and mortgages to finance private and apartment dwellings.

Public Health. As a result of modern medical practices epidemic diseases are rapidly disappearing from Mexico. Life expectancy is now 65 years.

E. THE ECONOMY

Mexico's economy has developed more rapidly and consistently than that of many of the other Latin American nations. While it has centered around agriculture and mining, industrialization has taken giant steps in the past decade. Industrial plants have been opened up in the poorer areas of the country in hopes of building a balanced economy.

Agriculture. Mexico is basically an agricultural nation with more than half of the population actively employed in agriculture and related fields. It is a country of small individual farms, collective farms (*ejidos*), cooperatives, and large, privately managed *haciendas*. Favorable climate and fertile soil allow wide diversification of products.

Corn and wheat are grown in the northern highlands and central states. The number one value crop and a chief export—cotton—is grown in Mexicali, Matamoros, and the Laguna area. Coffee, the nation's second most important crop, is grown near Vera Cruz and Chiapas. Cattle, sheep, pigs, and goats are raised throughout the country. Pineapples, rice, bananas, chicle (used in making chewing gum), vanilla beans, sugarcane and coconuts are grown along the hot, humid eastern coast. Mexico supplies more than half of the world's needs of *henequen* which is grown in the Yucatán Peninsula. The henequen leaves contain a fiber called *sisal* which is used to make strong rope and shipping bags. Vegetables are grown in the southern areas of Sonora, Sinoloa, and Tamaulipas. The value of tomatoes, lettuce, peas, and citrus fruits exported during the winter to the United States is considerable.

Coffee, cotton, and sugar are the most important export crops, in that order. High prices and good weather have moved coffee into first place in the last few years.

Although some farmers grow peppers, beans, onions, tomatoes, and other vegetables, the largest crop is corn from which *tortillas* are made. The farmer's wife crushes the corn kernels on a stone slab into meal to which she adds water to make dough. She rolls the balls of dough and pats them into thin, flat pancakes and bakes them until they are hot and crisp. *Tortillas* are eaten with almost every meal.

The Mexicans also eat *frijoles* (beans), *tamales,* and *enchiladas. Tamales* are made of ground meat, seasoned with chili, rolled in cornmeal dough, wrapped in corn husks and steamed. An *enchilada* is a *tortilla* filled with meat or cheese, rolled and served with a seasoned tomato sauce.

Most Mexican farmers are poor because the privileged classes have traditionally owned the land. However, in 1915, the government enacted laws to provide for more equitable land distribution by making some of the large estates or *haciendas* into community-owned lands called *ejidos*. The Mexican government has also given loans on easy terms for seed and fertilizer. Therefore, the majority of poorer farmers have become able to produce enough for themselves and their families, though they do not have any left over for the market. Most of the exports are still produced on the larger *haciendas*.

Mineral Wealth. Mexico has vast mineral deposits and nearly every state carries on some mining. Ninety-seven percent of the mines were owned by foreign interests until 1960 when the government passed laws requiring the sale of 51 percent of all foreign-owned stock in mines to Mexican interests.

Mexico is the fifth largest producer of silver. Other important metals are gold, lead, zinc, and copper. Iron and coal are mined for domestic use and are more than sufficient to support the heavy iron and steel industry of the nation.

Mexico ranks high in the production of sulphur, mercury, lead, graphite, zinc, and antimony. In addition cadmium, molybdenite, tungsten, tin, manganese, arsenic, and bismuth are also mined.

Manufacturing. While not primarily a manufacturing nation, industrialization in Mexico has maintained a high growth rate. Industrialization began in the 1880's when the railroads were built and increased in 1893 with the development of hydroelectric power.

Today, steel, textiles, and sugar are the largest industries, with the chemical industry, machinery for industry, agriculture, irrigation, road building, and oil production close behind. The change in Mexico's automotive industry from assembly to manufacturing has stimulated growth in production of plastics and chemical materials needed for that industry.

In 1973 the Mexican government passed a law requiring new investment projects to have a majority of their stock owned by Mexican interests. The only exceptions are to be investment projects required by the national interest, and a special board has been established to determine which qualify.

Foreign Trade. Most of Mexico's exports are sold to the United States, and Mexico is a principal buyer of American-made goods. The Joint Mexican-United States Trades Committee was set up in 1965 to reinforce the upward trend in trade. Mexico also maintains trade relations with Japan, West Germany, France, and Great Britain. Increased trade is developing with other countries of the Latin American Free Trade Association, and Mexico is seeking to develop a Central American Common Market.

Tourism. Mexico's largest single source of wealth comes from tourists—primarily Americans. The Tourism Council is aiding the government in building hotels and improving tourist attractions "south of the border."

Mexico City offers much of interest to tourists. Chapultepec Park was once the summer retreat of Montezuma and is today a favorite recreation spot. Xochimilco, the "floating gardens" near the city, is often called the "Venice of Mexico." The Shrine of the Virgin of Guadalupe is located in Mexico City, which is the center of industry, commerce, and culture.

Guadalajara, Mexico's second largest city, is a rich mining and agricultural area as well as a great tourist attraction. Mexico's famous ceramic industry is located here. Nearby are the Juana-Catlán Falls, the second largest falls in North America, and Lake Chalapa, Mexico's largest lake.

Puebla, Mexico's wealthiest city, is known as the "city of churches"; there are more than 60. Puebla is also noted for its beautiful colonial buildings.

Vera Cruz ("True Cross") is the site of Cortés' landing and is a combination of old Spain and modern Mexico. **Monterrey** is known as the "Pittsburgh of Mexico" because of its large iron and steel industry. The young men and women still carry on the old Spanish tradition of *serenalos*—strolling to the music of the city band.

Cuernavaca and **Acapulco** are Mexico's best-known vacation spots. Chichén Itzá in Yucatán and Teotihuacán, near Mexico City, are two of the better known ancient sites.

F. ECONOMIC PROBLEMS AND PROSPECTS

Mexico's most urgent problem is the low standard of living of most Mexicans. Though the per capita income of about $1,000 a year is higher than some other Latin American countries, half of the population lives no better than it did 50 years ago. The country's economy is better balanced, but the distribution of wealth is more uneven than it was years ago. The average Mexicans do not benefit, especially those who live in rural areas.

Land is another problem. Mexico recently completed a 50-year program of land reform, but the process of buying large estates and dividing them into small plots for peasants has been slow. Also, there is not enough land to go around, especially as the population has increased. Because of lack of irrigation, only 11 percent of the land in Mexico can be cultivated.

Money from oil and gas production, efficient government planning, and stimulation of the economy produced an economic boom in 1979. Despite these good signs the government has been trying to counter the pressures of inflation (slightly less than 20 percent). One method of achieving this goal was to further industrialize the economy by increasing production.

The promise of wealth held out by Mexico's oil reserves is a dangerous distortion, many experts say. Unless money from the sale of oil is invested in other areas of the economy to increase and diversify production, the oil will mean very little to the people of Mexico. The country has proven crude oil reserves of 45.8 billion barrels, enough to meet domestic needs for 60 years.

In the areas of social policy, Mexico's 1979 budget saw only 11 percent spent on health care and social security and 9 percent spent on education, science, and technology. These are all areas where Mexico needs to improve conditions.

Population proves to be a continuing problem as increases threaten the land best suited for living. Overcrowding in Mexico City and the central plateau of Mexico has prompted the government to encourage families to resettle in the humid tropics.

G.   RELATIONS BETWEEN MEXICO AND THE UNITED STATES

Relations between Mexico and the United States have cooled considerably over the past few years. Issues dividing the two countries are trade policy, energy prices, smuggling, and the influx of illegal aliens into the United States. Because of high unemployment and low wages in their own country, millions of Mexicans have illegally crossed the border and obtained work in the United States. The United States government has tried to stop the flow of illegal aliens and to encourage those present to leave. Mexico argues that it cannot reabsorb these people without causing economic chaos. It contends that the problem must be solved by easing trade restrictions against Mexican products, thereby allowing industry and agriculture to expand and create new jobs at home. The United States wants Mexico to lower its tariffs, but Mexico hesitates for fear that increased imports would harm its producers. In exchange for its support in halting the flow of narcotics into the United States, Lopez Portillo wants the United States to take steps to stop the smuggling of American merchandise across the border.

Mexican oil and gas reserves are attractive to the energy-hungry United States and other industrialized nations of the world. Closeness to the United States means lower transportation costs of oil for the United States. Beyond oil and gas, the United States and Mexico have much to gain from each other. Mexico is the United States' fifth largest trading partner with more than $9 billion in goods being exchanged.

QUESTIONS AND ACTIVITIES

KEY WORDS, PEOPLE, AND PHRASES

Can you identify and explain the following words, names and phrases? Use an encyclopedia or dictionary if necessary.

Baja California	Benito Juarez	José Lopez Portillo
Francisco de Cordoba	apostolic delegate	Yucatán
"grito de Dolores"	*ejidos*	bureaucrats

MULTIPLE CHOICE TEST

In each of the following, you have four choices. Choose the only correct answer.

1. The Mexican Indians who have been called the "Greeks of the New World" were the *(a)* Incas, *(b)* Toltecs, *(c)* Aztecs, *(d)* Mayas.
2. One of the reasons why Cortez found it so easy to conquer the Aztec Empire was because the Indians thought the Spanish were *(a)* demons, *(b)* gods, *(c)* chiefs, *(d)* animals.
3. In 1824, the Mexican Congress adopted a constitution which *(a)* freed the slaves, *(b)* granted titles of nobility, *(c)* gave freedom of speech, *(d)* granted freedom of the press.
4. Money from the sale of what resources produced a boom in Mexico beginning in the late 1970s? *(a)* silver and gold, *(b)* oil and gas, *(c)* tin and manganese, *(d)* iron and coal.
5. The greatest percentage of the Mexican population is *(a)* Indian, *(b)* Spanish, *(c)* mulatto, *(d)* mestizo.

6. Mexico's literacy rate is now about *(a)* 40 percent, *(b)* 50 percent, *(c)* 60 percent, *(d)* 75 percent.

7. The majority of Mexican people earn their livelihood from *(a)* mining, *(b)* industry, *(c)* sea resources, *(d)* agriculture.

8. The number one export crop is *(a)* corn, *(b)* cotton, *(c)* coffee, *(d)* bananas.

9. The most important staple food in Mexico is *(a)* wheat, *(b)* beans, *(c)* chili, *(d)* corn.

10. Mexico is one of the world's largest producers of *(a)* silver, *(b)* gold, *(c)* sulphur, *(d)* zinc.

11. Mexico's largest single source of wealth comes from *(a)* agriculture, *(b)* industry, *(c)* tourists, *(d)* mining.

12. Which of the following cities is known as the "Pittsburgh of Mexico" because of its large iron and steel industry? *(a)* Acapulco, *(b)* Monterrey, *(c)* Vera Cruz, *(d)* Mexico City.

13. Only 11 percent of the land in Mexico can be cultivated because of lack of *(a)* irrigation, *(b)* tools, *(c)* farmers, *(d)* fertilizer.

14. Most of Mexico's exports are sold to *(a)* Spain, *(b)* the United States, *(c)* Brazil, *(d)* Argentina.

15. Mexico's wealthiest city, also known as the "city of churches," is *(a)* Mexico City, *(b)* Guadalajara, *(c)* Vera Cruz, *(d)* Puebla.

THINGS TO DO

1. Draw a map of Mexico; include its neighbors, water bodies, and mountains.

2. On your map of Mexico color the three tropical zones of *tierras calientas, tierras templades* and *tierras frios.*

3. Research Project: Investigate the contributions of the Mayas to the culture and art of Mexico.

4. Research Chichén Itzá. Tell about the great pyramid, *El Castillo.* How long did it take to build?

5. Draw a picture of an Aztec temple and another of the godking Quetzalcoatl.

6. Present an oral report on the exploits of Pancho Villa and Emiliano Zapata.

7. Visit your local travel bureau and obtain Mexican travel folders and posters to use as a bulletin board display.

8. Debate: *Resolved*—Mexico is a satellite of the United States.

9. Prepare a report on the "Church Affair." Explain both sides of the argument and then give your own opinions.

6

CARIBBEAN AMERICA

The nations of Caribbean America have entered a difficult period of economic and political transition. In 1960, there were only three independent nations in the Caribbean. Today, there are thirteen independent nations in this region. The nations of the Caribbean face serious economic challenges in the near future. Some problems are related to the small size of these island countries, their overdependence on export earnings from one or two products, and declining foreign investment.

Economic problems have tended to weaken the political institutions in the nations of the Caribbean. In the case studies that follow, we will examine the past and present course of two Caribbean countries—Cuba and Puerto Rico. Cuba has been considered a model for development not only for the Caribbean, but for the entire Third World.

A.   CUBA: THE LAND AND PEOPLE

The Republic of Cuba is the largest island in the West Indies. It is about 700 miles long and averages about 50 miles in width. The island lies at the entrance to the Gulf of Mexico, about 90 miles from Key West, Florida.

Although most of Cuba is low, there are several mountain ranges: the Sierra de los Órganos, in the western province of Pinar de Río; the Sierra de Trinidad, in central Cuba; and the rugged Sierra Maestra, in the eastern province of Oriente. Cuba's coastline is irregular and provides many fine natural harbors, particularly those of Havana, Santiago de Cuba, and Guantánamo. Low marshes border much of the Caribbean coast, while high cliffs rise on the north side of the island.

Two river systems flow from central Cuba, one toward the northwest, the other south. The Cauto, about 150 miles long, is navigable for only half its length.

Cuba lies within the tropics, but the trade winds and surrounding water make its summers bearable and its winters usually warm and pleasant.

Because of its warm, even climate, adequate rainfall and fertile soil, thousands of kinds of tropical fruits and flowers thrive there. The wetter mountains are covered by forests that contain valuable trees; mahogany, cedar and royal palms are the most common.

The People.   The original inhabitants of Cuba were the Ciboneys, one of the Arawak tribes. By 1550, the population consisted of a few white families, a small number of slaves, and less than 5,000 Indians. The Indians disappeared through sickness and fighting. They left almost no trace among the population. African slaves became a major factor in the development of a plantation economy. Slavery was not abolished until 1880. By 1861, almost 47 percent of the island's people were black or *mulatto*. Heavy white immigration in the 20th century, and light skinned *mulattoes* counting themselves as "white" in census-taking, reduced the black population to 12 percent in 1953. Today the population of Cuba is just under 10 million.

Cubans harvest sugar-
cane in April. Cutting
cane is hard work, even
with the sharp machete.

Wide World

B. AGRICULTURE AND RESOURCES OF CUBA

Cuba's fertile soil, acres of level land that are suitable for large-scale cultivation, and agreeable climate have made agriculture the chief occupation. Cuba ranks number two in the production of the world's cane sugar. For many years Cuba's economy was based on this one crop. Recent efforts to diversify agriculture have resulted in producing the world's finest tobacco. Coffee, cacao and vegetables of all kinds are grown throughout the country.

Most of the Cuban people make their living from growing and processing sugarcane. Before Castro's revolution, the *colono* system was the traditional method of farming. A company owned the land and rented it to a farmer who hired laborers to do the work. Farmers were paid for cane they delivered to the mill.

Sugarcane is usually grown from stem cuttings rather than from seed, as most other crops are. A piece of the sugarcane or stem cutting is planted and new stalks grow from its buds. When the green sugarcane is from 12 to 18 months old, it is ready to be harvested. The stalks are about six feet high at this time. Laborers work in the fields cutting as close to the ground as possible with *machetes* or long, heavy knives. The sugarcane is

102

then transported to the mill. At the mill, the bamboo-like cane is directed through steel rollers which are very heavy and crush out the sweet, slightly acid juice. The juice is collected in huge vats and boiled down to thick brown molasses. Raw sugar is extracted from the molasses. The leftover molasses is made into rum, alcohol, and other products. The raw sugar is sent to a refinery where it is made into the sugar we find in our stores and use at home.

Tobacco is the second most important crop in Cuba. Some of the best tobacco in the world comes from the Vuelta Abajo district of Pinar del Río province in the extreme western part of the island. Young tobacco plants are put in the soil early in November and are harvested in January. Much care is required for this delicate plant, and often it is grown under the shade of cheesecloth stretched mile after mile to protect the tobacco from the strong sun.

Other crops are rice, corn, bananas, and citrus fruits. Cattle, sheep, pigs, horses, and goats are the principal livestock. Many Cubans keep bees.

The forests provide mahogany, rosewood, ebony, and various dyewoods. There is excellent fishing all year round, and sponge fishing is important off the southern coast. The Sierra Maestra has rich deposits of copper, manganese, iron, nickel, chromium, coal, gold, and silver.

C. HISTORY OF CUBA

Columbus discovered Cuba on October 28, 1492, about two weeks after he first set foot in the New World. Settlement did not begin, however, until 1511 when Diego Velásquez landed with 300 soldiers. Except for a brief interval of British rule (1762–1763), Cuba remained under autocratic Spanish control for four centuries.

In the 16th century, the Spaniards made Cuba the springboard for exploration. From this island Ponce de Léon set sail in 1513 for legendary Bimini and its Fountain of Youth; instead, he discovered Florida. Five years later, Hernan Cortés sailed from

Cuba to conquer Mexico. In 1539, Hernando de Soto set out from there on a gold treasure hunt in Florida and wound up discovering the Mississippi River.

Though overshadowed in economic importance by Mexico and Peru, Cuba grew rich from tobacco and sugarcane and came to be known as the "Pearl of the Antilles." The island was so prosperous that it was a favorite target of plundering buccaneers during the 1600's and 1700's.

Being more easily reached by Spanish military forces than most of Spain's other American colonies, Cuba could not join the liberation movements that sprang up throughout most of Latin America during the early 1800's. Instead, Cuba became a haven for French royalists who fled from the terrors of the French Revolution.

Cuba exploded in open rebellion against Spain in 1868. Led by Carlos Manuel de Céspedes, the Cubans fought 10 years for independence. The Cubans were not able to win their fight; however, they did receive many concessions from Spain. In 1895 there was another outbreak of fighting against Spain. The poet José Martí, a national hero of Cuba, was one of the leaders.

The *insurrectos* were ruthlessly herded into concentration camps where many died from hunger and neglect. The United States government protested this treatment with no success.

But when the United States battleship *Maine* was mysteriously blown up while on a peaceful visit in Havana harbor in February, 1898, the United States went to war against Spain. One of the provisions after this short war was that the Spanish give up Cuba and leave the island. American troops stayed and the United States established a provisional military government that lasted for 20 years. During the American occupation, under General Leonard Wood, roads and damaged public buildings were rebuilt, sanitation facilities were established, food was provided and spectacular progress was made in conquering the dreaded yellow fever.

In 1902, the military government turned the island over to the Cubans and Cuba became an independent republic under

President Tomás Estrada Palma. Under the terms of the Platt Amendment, the United States maintained the right to intervene in Cuba's future affairs in order "to enable the United States to maintain the independence of Cuba." These terms were incorporated into a treaty over the objections of the Cubans.

Lacking any tradition of self-rule, Cuba found the path of self-government difficult to follow in the years after independence. Bitter disputes between Liberals and the Moderates, as well as violence and corruption, characterized Cuban politics. The dictatorship of General Gerardo Machado (1925-1933), ended when a general strike was followed by an army revolt. The unpopular Machado was forced to flee the country. In September 1933, non-commissioned army officer Fulgencio Batista seized control and named Dr. Ramon Grau president.

The United States refused to grant diplomatic recognition to the Grau government. This made the Cuban leader more hostile towards the new administration of Franklin D. Roosevelt. Batista, frustrated by Grau's ineffective leadership, transferred his support to Carlos Mendieta. Within four days, the new government of Cuba was recognized by the United States. From 1933 until 1959, the real power in Cuban politics was held by Batista.

During World War II, Cuba acted in close cooperation with the United States. Cuba gained prosperity as it leased military bases to the United States, found a willing market for its sugar crop, and expanded the production of its important mineral resources such as manganese, copper, and nickel. As president, Batista ruled with moderation. Despite corruption, it was conceded that democracy and civil rights were respected.

In 1952, Batista declared himself a candidate for president but acted to take power before the voters could decide. Suspending the 1940 Constitution, Batista quickly put an end to the democratic tendencies that had been in development. Under his control, Cuba entered a period of great economic prosperity. The majority of the people, however, did not share in these benefits. Batista's high handed methods and arrogance created resentment and led to movements that plotted to oust him from office.

The Rise of Fidel Castro. Among those who detested Batista's tactics was an emotional, revolutionary, young lawyer named Fidel Castro, the leader of an unsuccessful raid against the Moncado Army Barracks near Santiago, on July 26, 1953. Many of the attackers were killed; some were captured and systematically executed by order of Batista. Fidel Castro and his brother, Raúl, escaped to the nearby mountains. The Roman Catholic Archbishop of Santiago secured a promise from the military officials that those rebels still at large would be given a fair trial if they surrendered, and that they would not be murdered. After the promise of a trial, Castro gave himself up.

At his trial, Castro accused the Batista regime of betraying the great mass of Cuban people. He used his trial as a forum to announce the objectives of his revolutionary movement, which from then on was called the "26th of July Movement." Castro proclaimed that his revolution sought social justice for farm workers and the unemployed, industrial progress, land distribution and a fairer distribution of wealth.

The judge sentenced Fidel Castro to 15 years in prison, but he served only a year and a half because Batista freed all political prisoners in an attempt to solidify his position and pacify his opponents. After his release from prison in 1955, Castro went to Mexico where he began to recruit and train a force to invade Cuba. It was there that Castro met the Argentine-born physician —Ernesto Che Guevara.

On December 2, 1956, Fidel Castro and 82 followers of the "26th of July Movement" landed on the eastern coast of Cuba at Oriente Province, near the Sierra Maestra Mountains. A Cuban naval vessel discovered them and called for reinforcements. The Cuban air force and a thousand soldiers attacked the group. Only Castro, Che Guevara, and ten other men escaped to hide out in the mountains. A few years later this small group of invaders formed the leadership for a guerrilla army of several thousand men.

Operating out of the dense woods of the Sierra Maestra, the guerrilla band attacked the Batista military. The morale of the government troops sagged lower and lower. On the other hand, Castro's hit-and-run victories inspired Cuban youth to attack the regime with widespread sabotage. Fires were started, trains derailed, and electric power plants destroyed.

In January, 1959, Batista was overthrown by a revolution led by Castro, who proclaimed himself premier.

D.   THE TRIUMPH OF THE CUBAN REVOLUTION

Castro Takes Power.   Fidel Castro arrived in Havana as the idolized leader of a victorious guerrilla movement. Many world leaders saw in Castro hope for democratic government in Latin America. The Cuba of 1959 was considered by many to be the most corrupt nation in the Caribbean. While Cuba had enjoyed prosperity under the Batista dictatorship, distribution of wealth was most uneven. Much of the island's economy was controlled by foreign investors, and organized crime and corruption were accepted facts of life. To many observers, Castro and his youthful supporters seemed to be the cleansing force that would reform Cuba and transform the republic into a model nation for the Americas.

In his first days in control, Castro gave no clear indication as to the direction he planned to lead the revolution. Within a short period, relations with the United States began to deteriorate, and by January 1961, the United States broke off diplomatic relations. There is disagreement over which side was at fault. Supporters of the revolution point to the weak reception given to Castro when he visited Washington, the denial of United States arms sales to the Cuban armed forces, opposition to agrarian reform programs, the refusal to process crude oil from the Soviet Union, and exile raids from Miami. Those who blame the Castro government cite the trials and executions of Batista supporters, the arbitrary application of the land reform law, Communist infiltration in government, and censorship of the press. Most importantly, the disintegration of relations between the United States and Cuba was total, and Castro turned to Moscow.

CASE INQUIRY: *Cuba's Economy in Trouble*

Discontent in Cuba under Castro's regime reached the break-ing point in early 1980. Tens of thousands of Cubans fled their homes to seek a new life in America.

> Crops are rotting in the fields. Cigar factories are closing. In-dustrial production is faltering and thousands of hard-pressed laborers cannot find work. Cuba's perpetually undernourished economy has taken another severe turn for the worse . . . and even President Fidel Castro has begun to acknowledge his country's problems. "We are sailing in a sea of difficulties," he recently told the National Assembly of People's Power. "We have been in this sea for some time and we will continue in this sea. The shore is far away."
>
> Cuba's current plight is largely due to the dismal yield of last year's cash crops. A quarter of the tobacco harvest was wiped out by disease—all major cigar factories have been forced to shut down . . . and sugar production fell more than 1 million tons short of the target. . . .
>
> Decay may be spreading into Cuban cities as well. Castro acknowledged that law and order were breaking down in Havana and said he would meet the challenge by expanding the police force and imposing tougher prison sentences. . . .
>
> Cubans have been especially frustrated since relatives from the U.S. began visiting. . . . [In 1979], more than 100,000 Cuban-Americans came with their success stories. "We've got every-thing we want," said one visitor. . . . [But] Castro can hardly turn the affluent tourists away. More than ever, Cuba needs their money.

1. What are the main reasons for Cuba's economic problems? Why are "cash crops" critical for a country's economic well being?

2. How has Fidel Castro responded to his country's economic crisis? What alternatives could he consider?

3. How could Cuban-American visitors have "sparked" the Cuban emigration to the United States beginning in April 1980? Do you feel that the United States government should restrict emigration by foreign refugees to America? Why or why not?

From "Castro's Sea of Troubles," by Fred Bruning, and Larry Rohter, *Newsweek*, vol. XCV, no. 9, March 3, 1980. pages 39-40.

Bay of Pigs. In the month that the United States broke off relations with Cuba, a new American president assumed the office of chief executive, John F. Kennedy. Within three months, the United States, through the Central Intelligence Agency, planned an overthrow of the Castro government. Using Cuban exiles as assault forces and Central America as a departure point, the Kennedy Administration hoped to replace Castro with a government more in agreement with United States interests.

On the morning of April 17, 1961, a force of 1,800 United States-sponsored Cuban exiles, trained and armed by the Central Intelligence Agency, landed on Cuba's southern coast. Most of the invaders landed in planes based in Nicaragua; paratroopers flown from Guatemala were dropped inland. Their task was to disrupt communications and prevent Castro's forces from cutting off the beachhead. Advantages gained by surprise were quickly lost when Castro's air force, which was supposed to have been destroyed by air strikes from Guatemala, appeared. Castro's planes shot down most of the limited air cover protecting the invaders and sank the supply ships sitting in the bay. The anti-Castro invaders were on their own; nothing was able to get ashore after the first day—no food, no water, no ammunition, no soldiers. It soon became apparent that the invasion attempt had failed. Castro had scored the biggest triumph of his career.

The failure of the Bay of Pigs invasion was denounced and American intervention in Latin America was condemned.

Recognition by the Soviet Union. Much has been written about Castro's leftist tendencies. His public announcement on television in 1961, that he was a Marxist-Leninist, seemed to confirm the suspicion. In fact, the traditional Communist party of Cuba, a party which worked closely in support of the Batista government, did little to support Castro before he came to power. At first, the Soviets were less than enthusiastic about Castro, and economic assistance was less than adequate. In September 1961, an appeal to have the Soviet Union recognize Cuban Socialism met with no success. Meanwhile, the United States had begun to exert economic and political pressure on Cuba in an effort to undermine the Cuban economy. In December 1961, Castro proclaimed his Communist identification and gambled that this admission would make Cuba acceptable to the Communist world and enable him to receive badly needed supplies. Within months, aid was forthcoming from the Soviet Union, and Cuba was treated as a "nation embarked on the path of Socialism."

The Cuban Missile Crisis. Accepted by Moscow and by the Chinese Communists, Castro began to solidify the Socialist structure on the island of Cuba. The old line Communist officials were purged and replaced by others who supported Castro. By October 1962, tension between the United States and Cuba simmered as the CIA discovered Soviet missiles on the island. While there is debate over the Russian intentions for placing the weapons in Cuba, it is apparent that Castro wanted them as a deterrent to possible invasion by United States Marines. The affair, now known as the "Cuban Missile Crisis," resulted in a complete humiliation for Castro and the Soviet Union as President Kennedy forced the Soviets to withdraw the weapons.

Cuba's Role in Latin America. In the shadow of the American threat and unsure of the Soviet commitment to Cuba's survival, Castro decided to export his revolution in order to insure the survival of his regime. Castro was soon to discover, however, that South America is not Cuba. In 1964, the Organization of American States imposed economic and diplomatic sanctions on Cuba for attempting to arm guerrillas in Venezuela. In 1967, another attempt to export revolution failed when Che Guevara was killed in Bolivia. During the 1970's, Cuba's approach to revolutionary activities became more cautious. Activities were tailored to suit local conditions. Cuba has attempted to extend and improve its relationships with governments that are democratic. At the same time it has kept its ties with leftist factions in those countries its considers reactionary. On a broader scale, Castro has sent troops to support revolutionary movements in Africa.

E. CUBA, THE SOVIET UNION, AND THE UNITED STATES

Cuban-Soviet Relations.   Twenty years after the success of the revolution, Cuba's relationship with the Soviet Union remains important. In 1979, Soviet economic support reached a level of $3 billion. Two thirds of Cuba's trade is with the Soviet Union. Much of the assistance is in the form of subsidies on Cuban products. In 1979, the Soviets paid 44 cents per pound of sugar compared to the world market price of about 10 cents. Soviet petroleum is sold to Cuba at about half the world market price. Without aid, Cuba's economy would be in serious trouble.

The Soviets have played an important role in maintaining the powerful Cuban military forces. Modern military equipment is provided to Castro without cost. The Soviets also maintain a combat brigade in Cuba of some 3,000 soldiers. This dependence on Soviet aid has been a mixed blessing for the Castro government. While the benefits are obvious, it has weakened Cuba's case as a leader of the non-aligned bloc of nations. Support of the 1980 Soviet invasion of Afghanistan probably lost Cuba the support of the Third World nations and a seat on the United Nations Security Council.

Relations Between Cuba and the United States.   Despite its ties with the Soviet Union, the Castro government is interested in expanding trade with the West and especially the United States. Without hard currency, purchases of technical and industrial goods are impossible. For a number of years, Castro has indicated that the United States and Cuba could find a way to resume normal trade relations. The United States has insisted that there could be no real improvement in trade or diplomatic relations until Cuba reduces what it sees as an aggressive foreign policy.

In recent years, the United States and Cuba have managed to open up lines of communication. The travel ban to Cuba has been lifted by the United States and certain Cubans are allowed to visit the United States. Given Cuba's recent attempts to intervene in the problems of Central America, it seems unlikely that relations between the two countries will improve soon.

F. CUBA, THE BALANCE SHEET OF THE REVOLUTION

The Cuba of 1960 and the Cuba of 1980 are very different countries. In a short period of time the revolutionary leaders of Cuba have transformed all of the major existing institutions into a Socialist state. Perhaps the most significant accomplishment of the revolution has been the emphasis upon equality for all citizens. Class, sex, race, and income distinctions have been eliminated or greatly reduced. To some extent this movement was fostered by the exodus of the former middle-income groups of Cuban society to the United States. On the other hand, the loss of this creative group has resulted in economic stagnation, waste of capital resources, and low productivity. Special attention to education and the campaign against illiteracy have had apparently positive results. Much of the teaching, however, reflects Marxist-Leninist thought and the cultivation of "correct revolutionary attitudes." Enormous strides have also been made to provide housing and medical care for the people of Cuba, and the vices of pre-revolutionary Cuba, such as corruption and violent crime, have been brought under control. Politically, Castro and a small handful of loyal supporters determine a policy that allows no challenge to its authority. In this respect, Castro is very much in the mold of the 19th century *caudillo*. Civil rights accepted in democratic countries, such as a free press and dissent, are not permitted. The arts are controlled by the government and much of the content is shaped to suit government policy. Trade unions have no real role to play in the decision-making process affecting their situations. In effect, Cuba has made advances but has also sustained real losses as a result of the revolution. By the middle of 1980, thousands of Cubans demonstrated their discontent with life in Cuba by fleeing the country. Others staged demonstrations in Havana pledging support to the revolution. It is still too early to judge the revolution. Perhaps the answer will come when Castro is gone. At that time the revolution will have become institutionalized, or the system will crumble with the disappearance of the *caudillo*.

G. THE ISLAND OF PUERTO RICO

In language, customs and traditions, Puerto Rico belongs to the Spanish culture of Latin America, but politically, it has close ties to the United States. It is neither a state, a colony, nor a territory. It is a commonwealth—"a freely associated state of self-governing United States citizens." The Puerto Ricans call this commonwealth *Estado Libre Asociado* or Free Associated State. Thus, the island of Puerto Rico links the Anglo-Saxon north with the Hispanic lands to the south.

The Land. Puerto Rico and the other islands of the Greater Antilles, rising out of the Caribbean Sea and the Atlantic Ocean, are formed by the high peaks of two mountain chains—the Cordillera Central and the Sierra de Cayey—whose bases are buried beneath the sea.

Aerial view of El Morro Fortress which guarded the entrance of San Juan harbor during the colonial era.

Puerto Rico Tourist Development Company

The island of Puerto Rico makes up part of the boundary of islands between the Atlantic Ocean and the Caribbean Sea.

The island is a roughly rectangular-shaped land mass approximately 100 miles long and 35 miles wide. It is largely mountainous, and its central mountain chain, the Cordillera Central, rises almost directly out of the sea on the western coast. Its highest peak, Cerro de Punta, rises 4,389 feet; it would be higher than Mount Everest if measured from its base at the bottom of the Atlantic Ocean. While 70 per cent of the island is rugged terrain, fertile coastal lowlands rim the island and form valleys between the mountains.

San Juan is the capital, chief port, cultural, commercial, and industrial center of Puerto Rico. This ancient yet modern city is located on a small rocky island north of the main island and is connected to it by bridges and a causeway. Its Cathedral of San Juan Bautista contains the tomb of its founder—Ponce de León. The massive fortress El Morro and the San José Church are other historic landmarks.

Modern buildings include the luxury beach hotels, the airport, and a campus of the University of Puerto Rico. Millions of dollars have been spent on its harbors to encourage one of its major industries—tourism.

A gourmet's paradise, San Juan (as well as other parts of Puerto Rico) is noted for its *arroz con pollo* (chicken with rice), *arroz con gandules* (rice, pork and pigeon peas), *cangrejos* (land crabs), and *lechón asado* (spit-roasted pork).

Ponce, on the Caribbean Sea, 45 miles southwest of San Juan, is Puerto Rico's second largest city. An important port and manufacturing and shipping center, this city was named for Ponce de León, the first Spanish governor of the island. Deeply influenced by Spanish culture, this city reflects its old world background.

Mayaguez, the island's third largest city, is situated on the west coast of Puerto Rico, 70 miles from San Juan. This rich agricultural region is the site of the College of Agriculture and Mechanical Arts, a branch of the University of Puerto Rico. In this area can be found extensive sugar, coffee, and pineapple plantations (called *fincas*), lush jungles, mountain valleys, and color-splashed vegetation of every kind.

H. A SPANISH COLONY

In 1493, Columbus landed in Puerto Rico and named it San Juan Bautista (Saint John the Baptist). One day in 1508 Ponce de León, looking for the Fountain of Youth, dropped anchor in a wide, beautiful bay and exclaimed, "Que rico puerto!" ("What a rich port!"). The island has ever since been called Puerto Rico. Ponce de León established the first stable settlement on the island near the present capital, San Juan.

The Spaniards found a tribe of Arawak Indians, a peaceful, agricultural people, already occupying the island. They were hospitable to the newcomers and even helped them discover gold. The Indians were expected to recognize the sovereignty of the King of Spain by paying him a gold tribute. They were also expected to provide labor to supply the Spanish with provisions. In return for this, the Indians were to receive Christian religious instruction. In 1511, the Indians revolted but were rapidly suppressed by the Spanish. The Indians were again forced to mine gold along with African slaves brought to the island by early traders. When the production of gold declined in the 1530's, the Spanish, using Indian and black slave labor, turned to agriculture. The Spanish colony was racked by plagues and ravaged by pirates. But Spain began to appreciate the strategic value of this island in the Western Hemisphere.

San Juan was converted into a well-fortified military post. Stone bastions were erected to command the narrow entrance to the bay. The fortress, El Morro, was built to dominate the harbor which became a refuge for friendly ships. Another fortress was built at the eastern end of the city to protect its Atlantic coast from plunderers. San Juan became almost unconquerable.

By the middle of the 16th century, Spain found it increasingly difficult to continue its "new world" policy of draining gold from its colony of Puerto Rico. Pirates roamed the shipping lanes and preyed on Spanish ships. Spain licensed privateers to seize the cargoes of its enemies. Smuggling became a major activity in Puerto Rico because ginger, hides, tobacco, sugar, cattle, and fruit from the island were in great demand.

From the 16th through the 18th centuries, other English forces unsuccessfully attacked San Juan.

Spain then instituted a new policy of liberal reforms in its colony. Immigration bars were dropped and commerce was permitted with the outside world. Trade with Spain increased, and agricultural production was stimulated.

By 1897, under pressure from island political leaders, Spain granted Puerto Rico a charter of autonomy which gave it some freedom to run its own affairs. One year later, the island was ceded to the United States as a result of the Treaty of Paris which ended the Spanish-American War. A new era began.

I. THE UNITED STATES IN PUERTO RICO

General John R. Brooke became military governor of Puerto Rico on October 18, 1898. For two years the island was controlled by the American army. A police network was organized to ensure law and order; roads and sanitation facilities were constructed; and a system of public education was established.

Civil government was begun in 1900. Many Puerto Ricans, however, were dissatisfied. Therefore the law was later amended to provide greater native participation in government. With the enactment of the Jones Act in 1917, a U.S. style government was set up with a governor appointed by the president and Puerto Ricans became citizens of the United States.

During the first half of the 20th century, new aqueducts, hydroelectric plants, railroads, highways, government buildings, public schools and hospitals were constructed. The population increased and the death rate decreased. However, the rate of progress was much slower than the rate of population increase, although not as tragic as in other Latin American countries. The United States' Great Depression of the 1930's had an adverse affect on Puerto Rico, too. It was not until 1948, with the advent of "Operation Bootstrap" that the island's economy started to improve.

In 1951, by an overwhelming 76.5 percent of the vote, Puerto Ricans voted for commonwealth status, a political concept that had been fashioned by the majority party, the Popular Democrats and Luis Muñoz Marín, the Governor. The United States Congress accepted the mandate and Puerto Rico became a Commonwealth of the United States on July 25, 1952.

The Commonwealth Government's legislative branch consists of a Senate and House of Representatives; the executive branch is headed by the Governor who is elected to serve a four-year term. He is assisted by a cabinet. The government has its own judiciary system. In foreign and defense affairs, the Commonwealth is represented by the United States. An elected Resident Commissioner, who has all the privileges of other members of the United States Congress except the right to vote, speaks for the island community in the United States Congress.

J.   COMMONWEALTH OR STATEHOOD?

The 1952 change to commonwealth status temporarily quieted a running quarrel among Puerto Ricans as to whether they should join the Union as a state or become completely independent. Commonwealth status, as a political solution, took into account the economic realities of the island. It provided free and easy access to United States markets and also exemption from federal taxes as enticements to investors. The island had never been subject to federal taxes in the past because of its status as an unincorporated territory. If Puerto Rico were to be granted statehood, it would still have the advantage of access to United States markets, but would lose the tax exemption. If it were to become independent, the island would not have to pay United States taxes, but would lose access to United States markets because it would then be affected like any other country by United States foreign trade regulations. Independence could also bring about the additional loss of federal aid, which is substantial.

The Puerto Ricans who desire statehood have united into the Statehood Republican Party which, since 1952, has become the number two political force on the island, though it is still far outnumbered by the pro-commonwealth Popular Democrats who have captured 60 percent of the vote in recent elections. The Statehood Republicans stress the advantages of being one of the United States with the special privilege of voting membership in Congress.

Commonwealthers, on the other hand, insist that statehood would destroy Puerto Rico's industrial efforts because of the imposition of federal taxes. They fear that statehood would cause a decline in the economy and the resulting loss of jobs. They do not want to weaken basic ties to the mainland.

In 1962, on the 10th anniversary of the commonwealth, President Kennedy and Governor Muñoz agreed that it was again time to consult the people of the island concerning further development of the commonwealth. A plebiscite was to be held so that the Puerto Ricans could express a preference among (1) a more fully developed commonwealth, (2) statehood, or (3) independence. Developing a procedure for conducting the plebiscite proved difficult, so in 1964 the Puerto Rican legislature established a United States-Puerto Rican Status Commission to "study all factors which may have a bearing on the present and future relationship between the United States and Puerto Rico."

The Status Commission set up the machinery whereby transition measures could be taken if the people chose statehood or independence; proposals for further commonwealth development were also prepared in the event that the people chose this.

Shortly thereafter, the Governor of Puerto Rico, Roberto Sanchez Vilella, sent a plebiscite bill to the island legislature. The Statehood Republicans, believing that they did not have sufficient voting strength to win, wanted to postpone the bill. Over their objections, Governor Vilella signed the bill into law and on July 23, 1967, the plebiscite was held. More than 700,000 voters went to the polls; 60.4 per cent of them chose Commonwealth status.

No discussion of Puerto Rico, however, is complete without examining the position of a significant group who demand independence. The *Independistas* argue that the status of Puerto Rico as a commonwealth is simply a disguise in order to create the impression that there is some form of autonomy. Any status but a complete break with the United States will result, in time, in a complete assimilation of Puerto Rico's culture, tradition, and language.

Independistas concede that commonwealth status makes Puerto Rico exempt from federal income taxes. They point out in response that three fourths of the island's industrial establishments are owned by United States business interests located on the mainland and that these owners transfer the profits gained from their investments back to the United States. Furthermore, they feel that Puerto Ricans are among the biggest customers of mainland products and services, and the cash payments made for such goods goes back to the United States.

Some of the more radical independence groups have been known to resort to violence. In the 1930's, members of the *Partido Nacionalista* embarked on a terrorist program which cost a number of lives. In the 1950's, elements of the same party attempted to kill President Truman and wounded several United States Congressmen. In the 1970's, another radical group, the FALN, continued violence on the mainland against targets they viewed as being against independence. On the international level, the *Movimiento Pro-Independencia* (MPI), has sought alignment with several communist governments. The MPI has gained Cuba's backing in the United Nations in an attempt to have Puerto Rico declared a colony of the United States.

K.   THE PEOPLE OF PUERTO RICO

With a population of 3.3 million living within its 3,500 square miles, Puerto Rico is one of the most thickly populated areas in the world. The United States has 59 persons per square mile; Puerto Rico has 976. Serious overcrowding is a major problem.

Nearly three-fourths of the population is of Spanish descent; 24 percent is black or mulatto. Small groups of French, Corsicans, and others of European origin also live on the island.

An overwhelming majority of the people is Roman Catholic, but other religious denominations are well established. While Spanish is the language spoken by most Puerto Ricans, the law requires schools to teach English a minimum of 70 minutes each day. All children between the ages of six and 14 must attend the free public schools. The curriculum offered in Puerto Rico is quite similar to that of the schools in the United States, with both academic and vocational subjects being taught. The University of Puerto Rico is the main center of higher learning; it grants degrees in many fields, from medicine to the arts.

While the basic culture of Puerto Rico is strongly Spanish, United States culture has made a deep mark. There are bull fights and cock fights; there are horse-racing, swimming and basketball. The Puerto Ricans adore baseball; they not only play the game but are staunch rooters for their local teams.

Puerto Rican young people enjoy the latest trends in American dancing and music as well as rhythms from their own Spanish heritage. The people attend movies and concerts, shop in supermarkets, and follow with interest the latest features in cars and fashions. They enjoy long sessions in cafés, the evening walk (*paseo*) and political debate. They love to gamble; there are numerous lotteries held daily.

Like other Latins, the Puerto Ricans love fiestas. To celebrate Epiphany (January 6), children gather grass and flowers for the camels of the "Three Kings" who come bearing gifts. Their religious processions are brilliant pageantry.

In recent years, Puerto Rican civic and government leaders, have become aware of the need to foster greater artistic and intellectual activity and recreation to balance the emphasis on economic growth. This concern led to the development of a program that Muñoz called "Operation Serenity." Puerto Ricans now have their own symphony orchestra which plays in plazas and parks around the island. It has also made possible the annual Casals Festival in May and June at which the world's finest musicians perform.

L.   PUERTO RICANS IN THE UNITED STATES

In the 1930's, low wages, seasonal work on plantations, and a sharp drop in sugar prices caused a serious depression in Puerto Rico. Many looked to the United States as a land of employment. But the Great Depression had also taken its toll on the continent, and jobs were not readily available. After World War II the migratory movement of Puerto Ricans to the mainland United States resulted in a yearly outflow of population that reached a total of 75,000 in 1953, then declined to almost zero in 1962. With economic opportunities improved in the United States, the migration movement again gained momentum and reached an outflow of 45,000 in 1970. After that, however, the flow was reversed, with a total of 40,000 "mainland" Puerto Ricans returning to the island in 1975.

The post-World War II movement of population to the United States was a main part of Puerto Rico's modern internal migration from rural areas to cities. Growth of the larger cities and population declines in many rural areas are marked features of modern life in Puerto Rico.

M.   ISLAND ON THE MOVE—
"OPERATION BOOTSTRAP"

In 1940, Puerto Rico was an impoverished, agricultural land with very few natural resources. Although agriculture had been the mainstay of its economy for centuries, the one-crop economy, sugar, could not support the increasing population. The island produced only half the food its people required. Per capita income was $120 a year; life expectancy was 35 years; illiteracy and unemployment were commonplace. Federal aid could do little to arrest the continuing economic decline.

Since 1948, the Puerto Rican government has been conducting a self-help economic program which former Governor Muñoz described as "pulling ourselves up by our own bootstraps."

A land reform program was started to give small plots to thousands of squatter families on easy credit. Annual profits from plantations controlled by the Land Authority, a government agency, were distributed among all employees. Sugar is still the main agricultural crop, but the island's limited farmland is now producing tobacco, coffee, pineapples, and other fruit.

Governor Muñoz and his advisors launched an extensive industrial promotion program to lure private investment capital to the island. Liberal tax and land concessions (including exclusion from federal taxes for ten years) were offered to potential investors. Government capital was concentrated on improving roads, public health, and education. Waterfront shacks and slum neighborhoods have given way to neat housing projects, new factories, and the latest word in resort hotels.

More than 2,000 manufacturing plants now dot the island. Per capita income is over $2,472—the highest in Latin America. The gross national product has more than tripled. Tropical disease and illiteracy have been virtually wiped out, and life expectancy is the same as on the United States mainland—71 years. The industrial plants continue to provide the main thrust to the economy which is growing at the rate of more than 10 percent a year—one of the highest growth rates in the world. The total value of the island's goods and services was over $10 billion in 1977-1978.

In 1949, the opening of the Caribe-Hilton—a modern, luxury hotel built under the auspices of the Puerto Rican Government and operated by Conrad Hilton—launched a tourism boom that still continues today. Harbors have been developed and many more resort hotels featuring pools, beaches, and shops have been built. Over one million visitors and cruise-ship tourists went to Puerto Rico in 1977-1978 and spent $482 million.

Puerto Rico's economic program has been so promising since "Operation Bootstrap" got under way that it has attracted the attention of several developing countries. The program may well become the model for others.

QUESTIONS AND ACTIVITIES

KEY WORDS, PEOPLE, AND PHRASES

Can you define or identify the following words, names, and phrases? Use an encyclopedia or a dictionary, if necessary.

dictator	Platt Amendment	Cuban Missile Crisis
Ciboneys	Fulgencio Batista	Jones Act of 1917
Marxism	Fidel Castro	commonwealth
censorship	Che Guevara	Operation Bootstrap

MULTIPLE CHOICE TEST

In each of the following, you have four choices. Choose the only correct answer.
1. Puerto Rico is classified politically as a *(a)* territory, *(b)* colony, *(c)* commonwealth, *(d)* state.
2. To which of the following island groups does Puerto Rico belong? *(a)* Lesser Antilles, *(b)* Bahamas, *(c)* Virgin Islands, *(d)* Greater Antilles.
3. The founder of Puerto Rico was *(a)* Balboa, *(b)* De Soto, *(c)* de León, *(d)* Cortez.
4. The commercial and cultural center of Puerto Rico is located in *(a)* Ponce, *(b)* San Juan, *(c)* Mayaguez, *(d)* Salvador.

5. Relations between Cuba and the United States became strained when Castro *(a)* refused to visit the United States, *(b)* announced that he was a communist, *(c)* denounced the United States, *(d)* executed political prisoners.

6. The Cuban Missile Crisis resulted in *(a)* a clearcut victory for Khrushchev, *(b)* Moscow's agreement to remove the missiles from Cuba, *(c)* disunity in the Latin American republics, *(d)* the loss of United States' stature in the eyes of the world.

7. Most of the people of Cuba make their livelihood from *(a)* bananas, *(b)* sugarcane, *(c)* tobacco, *(d)* coffee.

8. Cuba's trade gap has been financed by *(a)* the OAS, *(b)* the World Bank, *(c)* the Soviet Union, *(d)* American businessmen.

9. Efforts to diversify Cuban agriculture resulted in producing the world's finest *(a)* tobacco, *(b)* oranges, *(c)* pineapples, *(d)* cotton.

10. Two thirds of Cuba's trade is with *(a)* the United States, *(b)* the Soviet Union, *(c)* Puerto Rico, *(d)* Mexico.

11. The nation that maintains a combat brigade in Cuba is *(a)* Spain, *(b)* China, *(c)* Chile, *(d)* the Soviet Union.

12. In Cuba civil rights such as a free press are *(a)* permitted, *(b)* not permited, *(c)* allowed only in cities, *(d)* encouraged.

13. Puerto Ricans are citizens of *(a)* Spain, *(b)* the United States, *(c)* Cuba, *(d)* Mexico.

14. Some Puerto Ricans do not want their island to become a state because if they do their *(a)* men will be drafted into the army, *(b)* exemption from federal taxes will be lost, *(c)* United States markets will be lost, *(d)* tariffs will be raised.

15. Some Puerto Ricans want to become a state because *(a)* they will have voting representatives in the United States Congress, *(b)* there will be an increase in jobs, *(c)* their tariffs will decrease, *(d)* their federal taxes will go down.

16. Which term best describes the election in which the majority of Puerto Ricans chose to keep their commonwealth status? *(a)* a referendum, *(b)* an initiative, *(c)* a plebiscite, *(d)* a primary.

17. In an effort to foster greater artistic, intellectual, and recreational participation, the Puerto Rican government began a program called Operation *(a)* Bootstrap, *(b)* Serenity, *(c)* Muñoz, *(d)* Entertainment.

18. The migratory movement of Puerto Ricans to the United States resulted in a yearly outflow of population that reached a total of 75,000 in *(a)* 1944, *(b)* 1953, *(c)* 1970, *(d)* 1975.

19. Under "Operation Bootstrap," the Puerto Rican government lured private investment capital to the island by providing *(a)* cheap labor, *(b)* transportation facilities, *(c)* liberal tax and land concessions, *(d)* machinery for factory development.
20. One of Puerto Rico's greatest sources of income is from *(a)* molasses, *(b)* industrial equipment, *(c)* tourism, *(d)* petroleum.

THINGS TO DO

1. Pretend you are a newspaper reporter and write several headlines concerning the Bay of Pigs invasion. Take one of the headlines and write a news article on it.
2. Prepare a bulletin board display on Cuba by clipping articles out of magazines and newspapers.
3. Try to interview a Cuban and report to your class his or her feelings about Castro and the United States.
4. Research project: Investigate the ways in which thousands of Cubans have fled from Cuba during the past 20 years. Consider the loss this represents to Castro's government.
5. Pretend that you are leading a tour to Puerto Rico. List the attractions you would see and tell why.
6. Research project: Was the United States justified in taking possession of Puerto Rico in 1898?
7. Prepare an oral report explaining why you think Puerto Rico should remain as a commonwealth, become a state, or become an independent country.
8. Write to airlines and ask them to send you travel folders about Puerto Rico. Use them in a bulletin board display.

7

CENTRAL AMERICA

The region that we know as Central America is made up of the republics of Guatemala, El Salvador, Honduras, Nicaragua, and Costa Rica, and the British dependency of Belize. The republic of Panama is frequently included with this group of nations because of its closeness to the other republics, but was until early in the 20th century a part of Colombia. The entire area, including Panama, covers about 200,000 square miles, an area comparable in size to the state of Texas. The combined population of the six countries is about 21 million people. The racial composition of Central America reveals that the Indian influence is strong in Guatemala, while El Salvador, Honduras, and Nicaragua are predominantly *mestizo*. Costa Rica's population is mainly of Spanish ancestry, and Panama is composed of mixed racial elements.

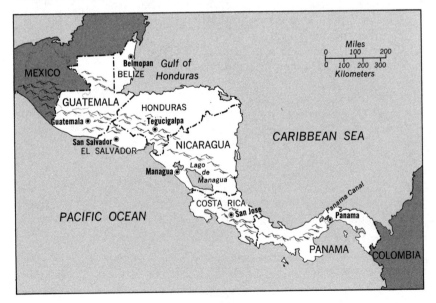

Topography. The land surface of Central America slopes upward from the jungles along the Caribbean coast to the mountainous highlands in the interior. In some parts of Guatemala the mountains reach heights of 13,000 feet. A separation between the mountain chains of Talamanca and San Blas on the isthmus of Panama makes possible the world famous interocean waterway, the Panama Canal.

Central America's location in an area of volcanic activity has meant that the people living there must often be concerned with the devastating effects of earthquakes. In 1972, Nicaragua was struck by an earthquake which resulted in the loss of over 6,000 lives, 20,000 injuries, and 300,000 persons left homeless.

Agriculture. The economy of Central America is based upon agriculture. Agriculture accounts for almost 90 percent of the dollar value exports in the region. Coffee, bananas, and cotton are the chief crops and these items alone represent 80 percent of the export earnings. Other crops that produce earnings include sugar and rice. With the exception of Costa Rica, political and social life in Central America and Panama has been under the tight control of a small elite group. Through alliances with the military, the elite have maintained themselves in power.

With its fast growing population and multiple problems of social inequality and economic dependence on agriculture, Central America is becoming a powder keg. The United States has historically dominated the Central American region and has supported numerous regimes. There are concerns that the unrest which has resulted in the overthrow of one regime in Nicaragua, and continuing civil war in El Salvador and Guatemala may cause the United States to intervene once again. Unlike the past, when intervention was justified in the name of the Panama Canal, this time, if it occurs, it will be to prevent the spread of Marxism from Cuba.

With its small size nations, Central America is often considered a microcosm of the Latin American experience. Nowhere is the contrast between nations sharing a common border greater than in Costa Rica and Nicaragua.

The natural resources of Central America include tropical woodlands which cover the greater part of the region (top), and hydroelectric power, such as this station on the Rio Lempa in El Salvador (bottom).

A. COSTA RICA—THE LAND

With a land area of almost 20,000 square miles, Costa Rica is just slightly smaller than the state of West Virginia. Its location in the tropics is affected by the presence of three volcanic ranges which gives the country a variety of climates. The Caribbean coast is marked by heavy rainfall and hot temperatures. Most of the population lives in the cooler highlands, where the capital city of San José is located. Because of the fertile soil enriched by volcanic ash deposit, agriculture is largely successful.

Unlike many other parts of Latin America, the *latifundia,* the *inquilino,* and landowning class never became a factor in the economy. Most of the farms are relatively small and are usually family owned. The chief crops are coffee, bananas, and cacao. These represent almost 95 percent of the country's exports.

B. HISTORY OF COSTA RICA

Costa Rica was discovered by Columbus in 1502, but it was not until 1564 that Juan Vasquez de Coronado founded the first permanent settlement. The Indian population welcomed the early Spanish settlers but later resisted and were killed or driven away to other lands. Costa Rica did not have the gold and silver which motivated Spanish interest in the New World. Consequently, the area was bypassed by the *conquistadores.* The settlers found it necessary to cultivate the crops themselves. A spirit of egalitarianism arose similar to that of the pioneers of the American frontier.

Coffee was introduced to Costa Rica in the early part of the 19th century. The fortunate combination of soil and weather produced a grade of coffee bean that is still regarded as among the best in the world. As an incentive to further production of the coffee crop, the government offered grants of land to any citizen who was willing to begin a plantation. As the coffee crop developed and was marketed all over the world, railroads were built and profits and government revenues swelled. On September 15, 1821, the five Central American colonies proclaimed their independence from Spain and joined together to form a united federation. The federation fell apart in 1838.

In the years after the collapse of the federation, conditions in Costa Rica proved uneventful as first coffee and then bananas became cash crops on which the economy depended. In 1866, free compulsory education was mandated by the government. Contrary to popular belief, however, political violence was not unknown. On a number of occasions in the 19th century dictators seized control. From 1889 to the present day, there have been two situations in which democratic procedures were not respected. During the period 1917 to 1919, there was a dictatorship under Federico Tinoco. A civil war was provoked in 1948, when Teodoro Picado attempted to manipulate election results to keep himself in power.

Today, Costa Rica claims the most democratic government in Latin America, the highest literacy rate in Central America, and one of the highest standards of living in Latin America. In 1980, when thousands fled from Cuba, President Carazo defied the Cuban leader and agreed to accept all Cubans who sought asylum.

C.   THE PEOPLE OF COSTA RICA

Costa Rica has a population of two million people. A large percentage of the population claim descendancy from the white Spanish settlers who came to the region in the 16th century. The relative lack of Indians in the area meant that integration along racial lines did not take place as in some other Latin American countries. Today, it is estimated that only about 20 percent of the population is *mestizo*, with an Indian population of about 3,000. There are also a number of blacks living along the Pacific coast. These Costa Ricans are descendents of migrants from the islands of the West Indies.

Class lines in Costa Rica appear to be far less rigid than in other Latin American countries. There exists a wealthy upper class, a middle class of professionals and shopkeepers, and a lower class composed of plantation workers. One does not find the class antagonisms that are prevalent in other societies, nor are there large numbers of people living in slums or on large estates as *peónes*. If there is a criticism voiced about the Costa Ricans, it usually concerns their reluctance to work more closely with their neighbors in Central America. For example there have been instances when unification conferences were called and Costa Rica did not send a representative. Criticism notwithstanding, Costa Rica enrolled in the Central American Common Market (CACM) in 1960. This organization integrates the economic structures of the region and works to create new trading opportunities for member nations.

D.   THE COSTA RICAN GOVERNMENT

In Costa Rican government most of the decision-making is carried out by the Legislative Assembly and the president. Elections for these positions take place every four years on a fixed date. In order to be declared president, the candidate must receive at least 40 percent of the popular vote or face a runoff election with the closest rival. The one-house Legislative Assembly consists of 57 elected deputies. Political participation by the people is widespread with an average of 80 percent of the registered voters going to the polls on election day.

The 1949 constitution has placed various restraints on the chief executive. One of these requires an outgoing president to wait until two four-year terms have passed before he or she can pursue reelection to office. In 1948, the Costa Rican military was abolished. To insure domestic order, a small Civil Guard of 1,500 soldiers is maintained.

E.   NICARAGUA—THE LAND AND PEOPLE

With a land area of 57,000 square miles, Nicaragua is the largest nation in Central America. Shaped in the form of a triangle, the country is divided into two regions by a mountain range. In addition to a number of swamps, volcanoes, and tropical forests, Nicaragua has the two largest inland bodies of water in Central America—Lake Managua and Lake Nicaragua.

It has 300 miles of coastline on its Caribbean side and approximately 200 miles of coastline on its Pacific side.

Nicaragua has a population of 2.5 million. Most of the people living in the more densely populated western region are of Spanish and Indian descent. On the eastern coast, the population is of Spanish, Indian, and Jamaican ancestry.

Like the other republics in Central America, agriculture is the basis of Nicaragua's economy. Among the most important crops raised are coffee, cotton, rice, and tropical fruits. Mining and cattle raising are also key economic activities.

Until July 1979, when the 46-year rule of the Somoza family was ended, the tiny elite of Nicaragua controlled 75 percent of the national wealth. The elite was made up of less than five percent of the population. During their rule, the Somozas became so well entrenched in the economy that it was almost impossible to distinguish their holdings from the assets of the state.

F.   HISTORY OF NICARAGUA

Nicaragua was discovered in 1502 by Christopher Columbus. In 1524, Granada was founded by Francisco de Cordoba. Spanish settlers soon arrived seeking the treasures of the Indians. The physical unattractiveness of the land, and the lack of gold, turned Nicaragua into a isolated outpost under the control of the Captain-General of Guatemala.

In 1821, Nicaragua joined Costa Rica and three other republics in Central America in the confederation of Middle American states. The union was short lived and ended in 1838.

Plans for a Nicaraguan Canal.   Shortly after the end of the confederation, Nicaragua became important to two world powers —Great Britain and the United States. Each was interested in building a canal across Central America to link the Atlantic and the Pacific Oceans. Nicaragua seemed to offer the best place for such a man-made waterway. The United States and Great Britain signed an agreement called the Clayton-Bulwer Treaty. This treaty provided for joint control and protection of a future canal. However, political instability in Nicaragua postponed the plans to build there. In fact, during a six-year period in Nicaragua, there were fifteen presidents — including an American adventurer named William Walker. As a result, the United States looked to Panama as a possible alternative for a Central American canal.

Despite the shift in United States policy to build a canal in Panama instead of Nicaragua, American interest in Nicaragua did not fade. Constructing a canal was one thing, defending it was another. To insure the security of the canal in Panama, the Bryan-Chamorro Treaty was signed in 1914. This agreement provided for payment of $3 million to Nicaragua and granted the United States perpetual rights to construct an alternative canal in Nicaragua.

Twentieth-Century Leaders. During the 1920's and early 1930's a new leader emerged in Nicaragua to challenge the established order. His name was Augusto Cesar Sandino. Sandino captured the imagination and sympathy of Latin Americans everywhere as he led a guerrilla movement against the corrupt government of President Moncada and eluded attempts by United States Marines stationed in Nicaragua to capture him.

In 1929, Moncada disbanded the army and created in its place a national police force known as the *Guardia*. The *Guardia* would be trained and led by American officers and would replace the Marines as security forces. The Marines left Nicaragua in 1933, and the new president, Sacasa, granted amnesty to Sandino in exchange for his pledge to lay down his arms. A year later, Sandino was seized by the commander of the *Guardia* and murdered. The *Guardia* commander, who two years later became president, was Anastasio Somoza Garcia.

During the period between 1934 and 1956, Somoza tolerated no opposition and gained enormous personal wealth. Somoza proved to be a popular friend of United States presidents who were concerned over Communist influence in the Americas in the post World War II era.

CASE INQUIRY: Nicaragua's War on Literacy

Although the young revolutionary government of Nicaragua is facing severe economic problems and food shortages, its plans to educate the people of the country have channeled the energy of teenage teachers to achieve a national goal.

> Every afternoon...in thousands of places across Nicaragua, in factories, city slums, churches, fishing communities, farming villages and mountain hamlets, 110,000 youths are teaching 700,000 people—a quarter of Nicaragua's entire population—to read and write.
>
> Not since the Cuban revolution two decades ago has such an ambitious literacy program been attempted in Latin America. . . .
>
> For many poor Nicaraguans, the campaign is also the first concrete result of the leftist Sandinist revolution that overthrew the Somoza dynasty. . . .
>
> One of the extracurricular duties of the teachers is to document the history and ledgends of the areas and to search for traces of pre-Hispanic civilizations. . . .
>
> The results so far, however, are highly encouraging. The drop-out rate among teachers is only 3.6 percent, and more and more illiterates are signing up for classes. . . .

1. Why is literacy a major goal of Nicaragua as well as other Latin American nations?
2. Why do you think the teenage teachers are instructed to gather information on the history and legends of the country?
3. How would you evaluate the effectiveness of Nicaragua's literacy program? What data or test results would you need for your analysis?

"Nicaragua Drafts the Young for a War on Literacy" by Alan Riding. *The New York Times,* June 3, 1980. p. A2:3.

Following the death of Anastasio Somoza, his relative Luis Somoza became president. In 1963, Nicaragua offered the United States military bases for an invasion of Cuba. Throughout the 1960's, the United States pursued a close diplomatic and economic bond with Nicaragua. Then, in 1967, a new leader assumed office—Anastasio Somoza Debayle.

G.   THE SANDINISTAS IN POWER

Shortly after taking office, Somoza encountered opposition from a band of guerrillas from the mountains near Matagalpa. Dismissing the guerrillas as nothing more than a band of Communist outlaws, Somoza sent his troops to seek them out and eliminate them. The guerrillas had taken the name of the *Frente Sandinista de Liberacion Nacional* in tribute to the patriotic leader General Sandino who was murdered in 1934. During the years preceeding his overthrow in 1979, Somoza allowed other groups to function to the extent that they were acceptable to his rule. With a firm control over the armed forces and an understanding with special interest groups, Somoza proved to be a very effective dictator. In order to show that his regime was "democratic," he allowed some political opposition but never to the extent that he felt a threat.

By 1978, the *Sandinistas* were operating out of bases in the neighboring countries of Honduras and Costa Rica as well as from secret military camps within Nicaragua. In June of 1979, the *Sandinistas,* enjoying the popular support of the majority of the people, were able to call a general strike which affected 80 percent of the businesses in the country. The revolt against the regime had become so widespread that in that same month armed clashes were taking place throughout Nicaragua. When a United States-sponsored proposal to send a peacekeeping force into Nicaragua was defeated by the Organization of American States (OAS) as interventionist, Somoza realized his power was coming to an end. In July 1979, he fled to Miami.

H. AN UNCERTAIN FUTURE

The actions that lead to the overthrow of the Somoza regime was a true reflection of the wishes of the people in Nicaragua. The victory of the *Sandinista* forces was achieved at a high price. More than 30,000 people lost their lives in the fighting, and the country was left in economic shambles. In an effort to establish good relations with the new government, the United States set aside $75 million to assist in Nicaragua's recovery.

Cuban Involvement. Cuba has long maintained ties with the *Sandinista* forces in their struggle against Somoza. Until the last major assault in the summer of 1979, Cuban aid consisted of military training, money, and granting asylum to *Sandinista* leaders. As the prospects for victory improved however, the Cuban government sent arms to the revolutionary army. While the help given by Cuba was a factor in the *Sandinista* victory, it was just one element. The revolutionary movement remained basically a national movement with historic roots in Nicaragua.

Since the revolution, Cuba has moved quickly and forcefully to assist the new government. By the summer of 1980, there were over 2,000 Cuban military advisors, teachers, and medical aides working in Nicaragua.

Aside from the Cuban foothold in Nicaragua, the United States government has expressed concern over human rights violations. These violations include summary executions, and alleged torture of political prisoners. There have also been efforts to censor the press.

The eventual resolution of affairs in Nicaragua is difficult to predict. However, similar popular movements are now taking place in El Salvador and Guatemala. The people of Central America are demanding certain rights and freedoms from their military-based governments. Even the Indians, who have traditionally been passive and unconcerned about national policies, are supporting guerrilla forces in Guatemala. Many view the *Sandinista* junta in Nicaragua as the first in a new series of popular revolutions in Central America.

QUESTIONS AND ACTIVITIES

KEY WORDS, PHRASES, AND PEOPLE

Can you identify and explain the following words, names, and phrases? Use an encyclopedia or dictionary if necessary.

powder keg	Augusto Cesar Sandino	Federico Tinoco
microcosm	Anastasio Somoza Garcia	Bryan-Chamorro Treaty
isthmus	Anastasio Somoza DeBayle	integration
inquilino	William Walker	Common Market
tropics	*peónes*	Belize

MULTIPLE CHOICE TEST

In each of the following you have four choices. Choose the only correct answer.

1. Which of the following is *not* located in Central America? *(a)* Costa Rica, *(b)* El Salvador, *(c)* Guiana, *(d)* Nicaragua.
2. Which country, now regarded as part of Central America, received its independence from Colombia? *(a)* Panama, *(b)* Costa Rica, *(c)* El Salvador, *(d)* Honduras.
3. Export crops are vital to the economy of Central America. Which of the following is a major crop of that region? *(a)* copper, *(b)* coffee, *(c)* tin, *(d)* tea.
4. Costa Rica is equivalent in size to which of the following states? *(a)* Arizona, *(b)* Texas, *(c)* California, *(d)* West Virginia.
5. Land reform programs have never been necessary in *(a)* Panama, *(b)* Nicaragua, *(c)* El Salvador, *(d)* Costa Rica.
6. Costa Rica is known for its political democracy. However one of its past dictators was *(a)* Tinoco, *(b)* Somoza, *(c)* Walker, *(d)* Sandino.
7. The name of an agreement intended to unify the economies of the Central American nations is the *(a)* Alliance for Progress, *(b)* Common Market, *(c)* OAS, *(d)* Good Neighbor Policy.
8. The capital city of Nicaragua is *(a)* San José, *(b)* San Salvador, *(c)* Managua, *(d)* Tegucigalpa.
9. One criticism of Costa Rica is that it could work more closely with *(a)* the United States, *(b)* Cuba, *(c)* other Central American countries, *(d)* Spain.

10. In Nicaragua, the Somoza family ruled since *(a)* independence from Spain, *(b)* less than twenty years, *(c)* almost 100 years, *(d)* over 40 years.

11. The agreement which gave the United States exclusive rights to build a canal through Nicaragua was the *(a)* Clayton-Bulwer Treaty, *(b)* Monroe Doctrine, *(c)* Bryan-Chamorro Treaty, *(d)* Panama Canal Treaty.

12. A Nicaraguan patriot who was murdered by Somoza was *(a)* Cordoba, *(b)* Walker, *(c)* Schik, *(d)* Sandino.

13. Guerrillas who fought against Somoza's army were known as *(a)* Sandinistas, *(b)* Fidelistas, *(c)* Tupamaros, *(d)* Guardias.

14. When Somoza fled Nicaragua in the face of the guerrilla victory he went first to *(a)* Cuba, *(b)* the United States, *(c)* Panama, *(d)* Iran.

15. As an expression of American support for the new government in Nicaragua the United States has *(a)* sent in Marines, *(b)* maintained a neutral position, *(c)* contributed money for reconstruction, *(d)* sent teachers and doctors.

THINGS TO DO

1. Read a book on the life of General Sandino. Try to decide if he was a great patriot or another *caudillo.*

2. Make a map of the countries of Central America. Using an atlas, identify their major resources, chief exports, and the capital cities.

3. Read an article about a Central American country and make a report to your class. *National Geographic* and *Americas* magazines are excellent sources.

4. Research project: Investigate the reasons why Costa Rica developed as a democratic country and Nicaragua as a dictatorship.

5. Debate topic: Resolved—The U.S. policy in Latin America is to support dictators.

8

SOUTH AMERICA

South America is a vast continent. It contains every kind of terrain from hot, steamy jungles in the Amazon to the snow covered peaks of the Andes, the longest continuous mountain chain in the world, and the world's highest lake, Titicaca in Bolivia. Some say the richest soil in the world is located in Argentina, and the finest quality nitrate is found in northern Chile. Ecuador and Venezuela have vast reserves of petroleum, Brazil and Colombia grow some of the world's best coffee beans.

South America is a storehouse of wealth. It is also an area of great political, social, and economic inequality. Poverty, suffering, and discontent exist alongside wealth, prosperity, and opportunity. The two countries discussed in this chapter are of interest because of their diversity, traditions, and history. Brazil is regarded by many as a super power in the making. Chile is attempting to recover from a stormy past which included the recent election and overthrow of a Socialist government.

A. BRAZIL—THE LAND

Brazil, the largest of the Latin American countries, gets its name from the red dyewood tree "brasil" that was used in the 16th century. This great triangular-shaped country has an area of about 3,290,000 square miles, and a population of about 118,000,000. On the north it is bordered by Venezuela, Guayana and French Guiana; on the west by Colombia, Peru, Bolivia, Paraguay, and Argentina; on the south by Uruguay. On the east it bulges into the Atlantic Ocean with a seacoast 4,500 miles long. Most of the people live along the coast.

A huge plateau covers the southern two-thirds of the country and slopes down to lowlands that form narrow coastal plains.

Even though more than 90 percent of Brazil lies within the tropics, the people are relieved from oppressive heat by the coastal winds, rainfall, altitude, and nearness to the ocean.

The Amazon Basin, near the equator in northwestern Brazil where few people live, and the tropical coastal plains have continuous hot, humid weather. A temperate climate is found in the southern and west-central areas of the country where there are sometimes frost and snow flurries. The Brazilian Highlands in the east-central part of Brazil have a warm, dry climate.

B.   HISTORY

Brazil was discovered in the year 1500 by Pedro Alvares Cabral, a Portuguese navigator who was attempting to sail to the East Indies. It is the only Latin American country where Portuguese is the official language. Because of the earlier Treaty of Tordesillas in 1494, it was claimed for the King of Portugal. Manuel I. Not until 1532, however, did Portugal establish its first settlement at São Vicente near São Paulo.

Brazil was divided into 15 captaincies or royal grants. King João III (1521–1557) hoped to speed up colonization in this new land in order to diminish the threat of French invaders. These captaincies, about 150 miles in length along the Atlantic Coast, were given to noblemen who had enough money to colonize the land, build towns and trade with Portugal. They could govern their royal grants as they pleased. King João's dream was short-lived, however, for the noblemen didn't want to settle in this new land. They returned to Portugal and left the colonizers to fend for themselves against the Indians.

Only two of these settlements succeeded, Pernambuco and São Vicente. King João was forced to appoint a governor-general to centralize the captaincies. Tomé de Souza, the first governor-general, was directly responsible to the crown. In 1549 he established the city of São Salvador in the captaincy of Bahia; it became the first capital of colonial Brazil. Under this system of governor-generals, colonial development increased rapidly.

The early Portuguese settlers hoped to find great mineral wealth as the Spanish had, but they were disappointed. So during the third quarter of the 16th century, sugarcane was planted along the northeastern coast on large plantations—*fazendas*. In a short time Brazil was supplying most of Europe with sugar. The settlers also developed a second important crop, cotton.

French Huguenots established a settlement on Guanabara Bay but were driven away in 1567 by Mem de Sá, the governor of Brazil, who later founded the city of Rio de Janeiro. In the early 17th century while Portugal (consequently Brazil) was under Spanish domination, the French Huguenots again established a colony in the captaincy of Maranhão but were driven out in 1615. In 1630 the Dutch succeeded in gaining control of seven captaincies including Bahia, but the Brazilians were ultimately able to dislodge them in 1654.

The Brazilian colony progressed quickly after 1640 when Portugal regained independence from Spain. The discovery of gold and diamonds in the late 17th century led to the opening up of the Mato Grosso, Goiás, and Minas Gerais. Most of the mines were within a few hundred miles of Rio de Janeiro; that city became the gold port of Brazil and later replaced Bahia as the colonial capital.

From 1750 to 1777 the Marquis of Pombal, known as "the great marquis," was dictator of Portugal; he governed Brazil with the best interests of the colony at heart. Most Brazilian governors, however, were cruel and oppressive. Their actions drove the people to seek independence and hastened the development of the feeling of nationalism.

In 1789 Tiradentes (Joaquim José da Silva Xavier) and his followers made the first serious attempt to establish a liberal republic. Their revolutionary uprising was short-lived for they were betrayed and finally executed. Tiradentes is still regarded as the leader of the independence movement in Brazil.

141

King João VI of Portugal fled with the royal court to Brazil when Napoleon invaded Portugal. João had refused to take part in Napoleon's continental blockade of England. He was greeted in Brazil with great enthusiasm by his colonizers, and he instituted many reforms for the betterment of the colony. He opened the ports of Brazil to all nations, encouraged trade, banking, and business; established the printing press and a Supreme Court; opened new schools and founded universities. Rio de Janeiro was completely rebuilt to be suitable for an emperor. In 1815 João proclaimed Brazilian equality with Portugal and became emperor of the United Kingdom of Portugal, Brazil, and Algarves.

With the defeat of Napoleon, the Portuguese government in Lisbon demanded that the royal family return or lose the crown. King João returned to Portugal in 1821, but left his 23-year-old son, Pedro, to govern Brazil as regent.

Pedro shared with his subjects the desire to be independent from Portugal. When he received orders to return to Portugal to complete his education, he proclaimed, "Independence or death" and separated Brazil from Portugal on September 7, 1822. He was proclaimed constitutional emperor, and Brazil was unified with the help of José Bonifacio de Andrada e Silva, Minister of State. However, when Dom Pedro dissolved the Constitutional Assembly for being too liberal, his subjects began to oppose him. They increased their opposition when their Uruguayan provinces were lost in 1828. Dom Pedro was finally forced to abdicate in 1831 in favor of his son, Pedro II, who was five years old.

For ten years a series of regencies ruled Brazil but failed to keep order. At 15, Pedro II, "Pedro the Magnificent," was declared emperor. He reigned for 49 years and succeeded in bringing about peace and the consolidation of his country. He increased Brazil's foreign trade and prestige, encouraged immigration, and boosted the economy by building railroads and encouraging the expansion of industry and agriculture. During his reign, Pedro involved Brazil in only two wars—to rid Latin America of dictators. The first, in 1857, found Brazil an ally of the forces in Argentina which brought about the downfall of Dictator Juan Manuel de Rosas. In 1865 Brazil allied with Uruguay and Argentina to rid Paraguay of Dictator Francisco Salano López.

Dom Pedro I had passed a law in 1831 to prohibit the importation of blacks as slaves. In 1850 slave trade was abolished by law. When the emancipation of slaves was proclaimed in 1888, the planters joined with the republicans and army to overthrow the emperor. On November 15, 1889, Brazil was proclaimed a Federal Republic; Dom Pedro was overthrown by a coup d'état and he returned to Europe.

C. THE GOVERNMENT AND THE CONSTITUTION

The Presidential System. On the national level the Constitution provides a presidential system with three "independent and harmonious powers": the president, the congress, and the courts.

Executive power is in the hands of the president, who, along with the vice-president, is elected by an absolute majority of popular votes for a five-year term. The president has the power to propose amendments to the Constitution and intervene in individual states if he determines it is necessary.

The legislative branch of the government is composed of the Senate and the Chamber of Deputies. The Senate is composed of 66 members—three from each state—all of whom are elected for eight-year terms. Two-year terms are served by each of the 409 members of the Chamber of Deputies.

The judicial powers are vested in the 11 Federal Supreme Court judges. The Federal Court of Appeals consists of nine members, and there are military, electoral, and labor tribunals. The jury system is used only in criminal cases.

In addition, each of Brazil's 22 states also has an elected governor and a legislature. Individual municipalities within each state elect a board of aldermen. However, such is the power and authority of the national congress and the executive that local government often is unable to exert much power or influence.

D. CONTEMPORARY POLITICAL SITUATION

Military intervention in Brazilian political affairs is well established in that country's history. The justification for such actions was based upon the belief that the civilian government lacked the ability to govern the nation satisfactorily. The last seizure of government was in 1964, against President Joáo Goulart. He attempted some radical reform programs that provoked the conservative military establishment to react with armed force.

Between 1964 and 1978 the office of president was occupied by military officers. The military enjoyed the cooperation of the business community within Brazil. By not involving itself too deeply in the day-to-day operations of business and public affairs, the military was also successful in obtaining acceptance among large numbers of the middle class.

While in power, the military did not react kindly to those who found fault with government policies. Censorship, arrests, and the torture of opponents to the regimen was common. In theory, provision was made by the military to give the appearance that their rule was legal. The national legislature, for example, was allowed to offer criticism of government programs. The president, however, was given constitutional power to disregard criticism or counsel from the legislature.

The regime did establish two political parties which prepared the way for the 1978 elections and the restoration of civilian rule. Those parties were the *Alianca Revolucionaria Renovadora* (ARENA), and the opposition, *Movimiento Democratico Brasileiro* (MDB).

Despite the government's firm control, there was discontent with the political system instituted by force. Students, in particular, protested the restrictive policies of the administration and demanded reforms. By June 1978, press censorship, in effect for almost ten years, was ended. In November of the same year, general elections were permitted. In those elections, ARENA, the government sponsored party, won a majority of seats in both houses of Congress. Brazil's Electoral College, composed of Congress and representatives of the various state assemblies, elected João Baptista da Figueiredo to be the next president. The outgoing military president, Geisel, made clear that Figueiredo was his personal choice as chief executive. On March 15, 1979, President Figueiredo was inaugurated as president of Brazil.

D. THE PEOPLE AND THEIR CULTURE

Brazil is a large country. In total land size it is surpassed only by the Soviet Union, Canada, China, and the United States. It is one half the land mass of the South American continent and three times the size of the next largest South American nation, Argentina.

The population of Brazil is a blend of many nationalities. Of a total population of about 118 million, approximately 62 percent are of European ancestry (mainly Portuguese), 11 percent are black, and 28 percent are of mixed origin, and 10 percent are Orientals. There is a relatively small number of Indians left—most of whom inhabit the dense rain forests of the Amazon Basin. The pre-Columbian Indians of Brazil had not reached a high degree of civilization when the Portuguese arrived. This fact, coupled with the great number of individual tribes and the lack of unity of the tribes, accounted for the ease with which the Europeans were able to conquer this land. Moreover, vast numbers of Indians died—and are still dying—when exposed to European diseases from which they have no natural immunity. This accounts for the small number of Indians left today as well as the reason why so many millions of slaves were imported from Africa to work Brazil's mines and plantations.

The culture of this great country is a combination of the influences of its Indian, European, and African heritages. The early black Africans contributed many elements to the already existing folklore of the Brazilian Indians and the early settlers.

With its high immigration rates and great diversity of people, Brazil is often considered an example of successful racial integration and intermarriage. In reality, however, there are sometimes conflicts and prejudice, based upon economic and social differences, if not specifically on race. In general there are relatively few blacks among the highest economic and social classes in Brazil.

There are relatively few people of Indian background among the leaders, political and social, of the nation. A few years back it was discovered that much of the Indian population had been decimated, both by murder and by the intentional introduction of disease into communities. Although this action was condemned, it could not be undone.

More than 90 percent of Brazilians are Roman Catholic, but the influence of the Church is not so strong as in other South American nations. Freedom of worship is guaranteed by the Constitution, which allows legal separation but forbids divorce.

Carnival, the biggest Brazilian fiesta, is a four-day pre-Lenten celebration which ends on the eve of Ash Wednesday. Carnival is very gay with songs, dances, balls, costumes, and parades. Rio de Janeiro is most noted for Carnival and all segments of society take an active part in it.

Education. Today the educational system of Brazil is based on regulations set forth in the Constitution.

1. Public elementary education is compulsory and free.

2. Public education on the secondary level is provided free to those who can show lack of means.

3. Academic freedom is guaranteed.

4. The federal government must provide a minimum of 10 percent of tax revenues yearly for education while the states must contribute not less than 20 percent annually.

5. When there are deficiencies the federal government must supplement state educational systems.

Elementary education consists of a five-year course; a student must attend for three. Secondary education includes courses in technical, agricultural, commercial, and specialized schools. Brazil now has more than 50 universities. The states are responsible for the training of teachers.

Adult education courses are given in hygiene, nutrition, home economics, sanitation, simple agriculture, reading and writing.

According to the Law of Direction and Bases, passed in 1961, each state has the right to form its own system of education, with only a minimum of curriculum requirements required by the federal government.

Many children who live away from the cities do not receive even the compulsory minimum of education. Schools must be built and teachers must be trained to educate all of Brazil's young people. Brazil has a literacy rate of about 83 percent.

E.   HOUSING AND PUBLIC HEALTH

Housing.   Brazil's population is growing rapidly. São Paulo is the fastest growing city in the world. Experts estimate that Brazil's population will double over the next twenty-five years. Population pressures mean greater demands on all aspects of public services. And one of the most critical needs, especially in Brazilian cities, is adequate housing.

The living conditions of the *favelas* (shantytowns) create severe problems. Landslides occur frequently on the hills where the *favelas* are located. Sometimes entire neighborhoods are washed away in the heavy tropical rains. These slums are made from boards, stone, corrugated tin, even cardboard. The contrast between rich and poor is most striking in cities like Rio de Janeiro. Rio's *favela* population numbers about 850,000.

People from the poor outlying rural areas *(sertao)* crowd into the cities in search of jobs and better opportunities for themselves and their children. As unbelievably bad as the living con-

Construction of a new reservoir in the suburbs of Sao Paulo provided piped water for nearly half the population in the city.

ditions are in the *favelas,* they are worse in the rural backlands. Recently, the Brazilian government has been constructing low-cost apartment housing in the urban centers. These new housing complexes will provide better homes for the poor and the rural migrants.

Public Health. The Ministry of Labor and Social Welfare is charged with all social programs for improving the Brazilian standard of living. It is responsible for labor, social security, public health, and all other social services.

Public health work is carried on by federal, state and municipal governments through the Special Public Health Service Foundation (FSEP), National Department of Health, the Oswaldo Cruz Institute and the National Children's Department. The FSEP is concerned with water supply projects, especially in backward areas, and community health programs. Under the auspices of the FSEP some 14,200,000 urban dwellers had an available water supply by 1964. Brazil has entered into an agreement with the Pan American Health Organization (part of

148

the OAS program of Technical Cooperation) for the planning of other water supply systems. By an Alliance for Progress agreement millions of dollars are earmarked for financing water systems where impure water is creating added hazards in cities already overcrowded and plagued with disease.

F. IMPORTANT CITIES

Brasília. For years Brazilians planned to build a capital city in the heartland of their country. In an effort to populate the interior and to expand the economic development of that area, the capital city was built 600 miles inland at a cost of over $600 million. During the administration of Juscelino Kubitschek the federal capital was officially moved from Rio de Janeiro to Brasília. At 300 feet above sea level, the new city enjoys a temperate climate.

Lucio Costa and Oscar Niemeyer designed the ultra-modern buildings. This growing city now has a population of over 700,000. It boasts a model university, three television stations, banking and commercial facilities, and all the cultural attractions of a nation's capital. Brasília is linked to the country's other large cities by air and road.

Rio de Janeiro. Capital of the State of Guanabara, Rio is the chief intellectual city of the nation and a center of international tourism. It was the federal capital from 1763 to 1960. Known as the "wonder city" for its unsurpassed beauty, Rio faces Guanabara Bay with Sugar Loaf Mountain at its entrance. Rio's population is almost five million.

Belém. This city is the gateway to the Amazon region and the capital of the State of Pará; it has a population of a half million people. Only 60 miles below the equator, Belém is continuously cooled by trade winds and frequent rains.

São Paulo. Capital of the State of São Paulo in the heart of the Brazilian highlands, São Paulo is the largest industrial center of

Latin America and the fastest growing city in the world. It produces almost half of all the income from industry in the whole country. With a population of over 7 million, its inhabitants take pride in being known as "Paulistas."

Recife.   This city, in the State of Pernambuco, is the "capital" of the Brazilian northeast, and the third largest city in Brazil. With a population of over 1 million, it is the distributing point for the northeast area.

Salvador.   Over 1 million people live in this the first capital of Brazil. It is also the capital of the oil and cocao-producing State of Bahia. It is the only Brazilian city with the majority of its population of African descent.

Belo Horizonte.   The capital of Minas Gerais, the richest state in mineral reserves, has a population of over 1 million. This modern city is destined to become one of the most important cities on the continent because it has so many vital industries— the manufacture of all types of clothing and furniture as well as cement, iron and steel products.

Recife, the largest urban center in northeastern Brazil, has a fine natural harbor and modern port facilities.

Varig Airlines Photo

G.   ECONOMY AND AGRICULTURE

Historically, Brazil's economy has been based on a one-crop agriculture—coffee—and a land-owning aristocracy. Other commodities were brazilwood, livestock, sugar, gold, and rubber.

Coffee is grown on small plantations on mountain slopes from 3,000 to 7,000 feet above sea level. The combination of red fertile soil, abundant rainfall, and mild temperature makes coffee trees flourish. Mature coffee trees are generally from seven to twelve feet high. The trees bear flowers which turn into red coffee berries about seven months later. Coffee is harvested almost all year round. It is not unusual to see flowers, buds and berries all on the same tree. Men, women and children work picking the ripe berries. Women and children pick from the lower branches and men use ladders to reach the higher branches. The berries are then taken to the *fazenda* (plantation) warehouse to be washed and spread out in the sun to dry. Workers rake over the berries regularly until they are dry. This may take days or sometimes weeks. When completely dry, the berries are put into a machine which removes the outer husks. The beans are then bagged according to size and stored in a warehouse until shipped to world markets.

Brazil's coffee-growing area extends from the northeast section of the country to the southern states of São Paulo and Paraná, and from the Atlantic coast to the western State of Mato Grosso—more than a million square miles. More than half of Brazil's labor force (6.5 million people) is employed in the production of coffee. Coffee exports add over $2 billion annually to the Brazilian economy.

At one time Brazil supplied 70 percent of the world's coffee. But since World War I, coffee-growing in other Latin American countries has dropped the percentage.

Coffee was first exported to the United States in 1809. The United States buys about 50 percent of Brazil's coffee today. The average adult American drinks at least three cups of coffee daily which adds up to millions and millions of cups. The billion dollar-a-year outlay for coffee stimulates economies in both countries.

Cotton is Brazil's second largest economy item. When the value of coffee drops, Brazilian farmers plant cotton to make up for lost profits. Brazil is one of the world's largest producers of cotton. It is grown mainly in northern Brazil, but is now being grown to a much greater extent in the south.

The cultivation of sugarcane began with the earliest settlements in Brazil. Now the third largest economy item, about 5 million tons of sugar are produced annually. At one time Brazil supplied most of Europe's sugar. The exportation of sugar today is relatively slight; the greater part of it is consumed in Brazil.

One of Brazil's largest export items is cacao, most of which is bought by the United States. The State of Bahia produces 95 percent of the country's cacao crop in an area of 1.1 million acres. Brazil is also the major producer and exporter of processed cacao products.

Chief among grain crops are corn, rice and wheat. Corn is grown primarily for domestic use. Brazil is the world's greatest producer of manioc, most of which is used by the Brazilians. Beans are a favorite national dish. Brazil also ranks high in the production of tobacco and is a major producer of fibers, vegetable oil and waxes, beverage crops and animal products. Livestock is an important traditional economy item; today, the Ministry of Agriculture imports pure-bred, early maturing breeds of cattle for crossing with native stock.

Industry. In the last 45 years, the Brazilian economy has become greatly diversified and industrialized. Industry has reached a high level of technical precision; most manufactured and semi-manufactured goods are produced from domestic raw materials. Over the years, automobile production has climbed to make Brazil the tenth largest producer in the world.

Brazil's industrial complex includes the manufacture of paper, cotton and cellulose textiles, plastics, elevators, telephone and communications equipment, precision instruments, glass, and crystal objects. In addition, Brazil produces large quantities of engines, synthetic rubber, wine, packaged meat, dairy products, cigarettes and cigars, chemical and pharmaceutical goods and fertilizer. Brazil ranks high in the world's production of sewing machines, and manufactures refrigerators, mixers, washing machines, transistor radios, and television sets.

H.   NATURAL RESOURCES AND FOREIGN TRADE

Natural Resources.   The forests of Brazil are probably the richest in the world. Their oil-bearing fruits, gums, resins, waxes, timber and fibers make Brazil one of the great suppliers of vegetable raw materials. About 1,350,000 square miles of forests produce lauric acid, Brazil nuts, peanuts, cottonseed, linseed, china wood, carnauba wax (used in the making of dynamite and phonograph records), and fine quality timber, especially the Parana pine.

The country has rich mineral resources, many of which have not yet been exploited. It has some of the largest iron ore deposits in the world, and its reserves of manganese are the largest in the hemisphere. In addition to gold, coal, zircons, and quartz, Brazil has substantial deposits of tungsten, bauxite, nickel, mica,

Construction of the Amazon Highway has opened new lands for agricultural use. Transportation has played an important role in Brazil's economic development.

United Nations/V. Bibic

lead, zinc, silver and uranium. The precious and semi-precious stones include diamond, emerald, aquamarine, beryl, garnet, topaz, tourmaline, andalusite and amethyst. The *carbonado,* or black diamond, is widely used for industrial purposes. Brazil leads South America in the use of atomic energy. Research is being made into the use of atomic energy in the application of isotopes to agricuture.

Foreign Trade. Brazil exports coffee, iron ore, soy products, cocoa beans, transportation equipment, machinery, and footwear. The country imports wheat, crude oil, machinery, fertilizers, chemical products, and motor vehicles, but in much smaller quantities than a decade ago. Brazil's principal trade partners are the United States, Argentina, West Germany, Venezuela, France, the United Kingdom, Japan and Italy.

I.   CHILE—THE LAND

The Republic of Chile is located along the southwestern coast of the continent of South America. Because of its shape it is sometimes called the "shoestring country." This is because while Chile has a total length of some 2,700 miles, its width never exceeds more than 200 miles. Chile is bordered on the north by Peru, on the east by Bolivia and Argentina, and on the west by the Pacific Ocean. Beyond its territorial limits on the continent of South America, Chile claims a large portion of the Antarctic, and the Juan Fernandez Islands and Easter Island in the Pacific Ocean. With the waters of the Pacific Ocean at its back, the driest desert in the world, the Atacama in the north, and the tall peaks of the Andes Mountains on the west, Chile merits the title of the "Lone Star Republic."

Chile has varied climates: the dry desert zone of the north (where no precipitation has ever been recorded in some parts), the Mediterranean climate of the central area, and the cold and rainy south. Almost 60 percent of the national territory is un-inhabited and about 70 percent of the population lives in the central or temperate zone of the nation.

J. HISTORY OF CHILE

The relatively easy conquest of the Aztec and later, the Inca, gave the Spanish *conquistadores* a sense of invincibility in combat. Cortés and Pizarro demonstrated that with horses and technology a small troop of soldiers could overcome the advantage of larger numbers. It was no surprise therefore that Diego de Almagro set out from Peru in 1535, with an army of less than 600 Spaniards and several thousand Indians to conquer Chile. Instead of finding gold, Almagro met the difficult geographic terrain, and a tribe of Indians, the Araucanians, who resisted the invaders. Pedro de Valdivia organized yet another expedition into Chile in 1540. On February 12, 1541 Valdivia founded Santiago, the present capital of Chile. However, Valdivia and his forces were defeated by the Araucanians led by a legendary chief named Lautaro. Lautaro had determined the best strategy for overcoming the advantages that the Spanish had used in previous combat with other Indian forces. His strategy was to relentlessly attack the small numbers of *conquistadores* until they became too exhausted to continue the battle. The heroic resistance of the Araucanians forced later Spanish armies to accept the Bío-Bío River as a boundary.

The Chileans were among the first of the Latin Americans to resist Spanish royalist rule. Early attempts at rebellion were crushed, however. In 1814, a group of patriots were defeated at Rancagua and prospects for independence were dim. The Argentine leader José de San Martín came to realize that no liberation of America could be won without a victory in Chile. San Martín led his troops across the Andes into Chile where they joined forces with the soldiers of the Chilean leader, Bernardo O'Higgins. Together, they defeated the royalists at Chacabuco in 1817.

With Chile secure, it became possible to continue northward to aid in the liberation of Peru. O'Higgins became Supreme Director of Chile, but despite his gallant efforts, the instability of the country proved to be more than even he could control and he was forced into exile in 1823. In the years following O'Higgins' exile, Chile experienced continued internal troubles and civil war. Chile found stability under the leadership of Diego Portales who was responsible for the 1833 Constitution. This document gave the president *caudillo*-like powers. The years after 1830 were marked by economic progress and internal peace. Relations between Chile and its neighbors Bolivia and Peru were not so peaceful. A federation between these countries was seen as a threat, and after a short war, Chile gained victory. In 1873, Peru and Bolivia again joined forces, this time under the terms of a secret agreement. A dispute over nitrate in the rich northern desert provoked a Chilean armed action in what has come to be known as the 1879 War of the Pacific. Chile scored a battlefield and naval triumph over the allied armies of Peru and Bolivia and emerged from the war as the most powerful nation on South America's western coast. Under the terms of the treaty ending the war, Bolivia lost the port city of Antofagasta.

The order within Chile made possible by President Portales gave way to a power struggle between those who favored strong executive power and those who championed parliamentary supremacy. The matter was resolved in the civil war of 1891. In this struggle, the President, Balmaceda, took his life and the congressional forces won. Congressional victory was marked by a period of ineffective government and finally the collapse of civilian government. The collapse was followed by military intervention, and a new constitution was drafted in 1932. Chile, so powerful after the 1891 war, became shaken by the political instability following victory. Its economy was dealt a blow by the development of synthetic nitrate.

Chile prospered during World War II, as the United States sought to obtain important strategic materials such as nitrate and copper. By the mid-1960's, Chile witnessed efforts by the Socialist-oriented "People's Action Front" and the Christian Democrats to gain government control. In 1964, the Christian Democrats triumphed over a popular front led by Salvador Allende. The Christian Democrats under Eduardo Frei advocated agrarian reform and the nationalization of the copper

CASE INQUIRY: *People's Power in Chile*

The following selection is an excerpt of the party program of the Unidad Popular written by Salvador Allende, former President of Chile.

> The revolutionary changes which the country needs can be brought about only if the Chilean people take power into their own hands and wield it in a real and effective way. After a long series of struggles, the people of Chile have won for themselves certain freedoms and guarantees of democracy for whose preservation they should be constantly on the alert and ready to fight ceaselessly in their defence. Real power itself, however, still lies beyond their reach.
>
> The popular and revolutionary forces have not united to fight merely in order to substitute one President of the Republic for another, nor even to replace one party by others in government, but to bring about those basic transformations which the national situation demands. These changes will be effected by transferring power from the old ruling groups to the workers, to the peasants and to progressive elements of the middle class in the city and in the country.
>
> The triumph of the people will thus open the way for the most democratic government in the history of the country. The problems of political structure that will concern the government are:
>
> —to preserve and make more effective and far-reaching the democratic rights and the triumphs of the workers.
>
> —to transform the existing institutions in order to establish a new state where power will truly belong to the workers and to the people.

1. What do you think is meant by this statement, "The revolutionary changes which the country needs can be brought about only of the Chilean people take power into their own hands. . . ?"

2. What hint is there in the passage that the Unidad Popular is planning to achieve more than winning an election?

3. How do you think the Unidad Popular planned to "transfer power from the old ruling groups. . . ?"

4. Based on the message contained in this selection do you think change in Chile could have occurred without violence? Give reasons to support your answer.

Salvador Allende. *Chile's Road to Socialism.* Penguin Books. 1973. p. 31.

industry. This plan pleased few and resulted in a hardening of political battle lines between the contending factions in the important elections of 1970.

K.   THE PEOPLE OF CHILE

Chile's ten million people are mainly a blend of Spanish and Araucanian Indian. In the southern areas of Chile, south of the Bío-Bío River and around Temuco, one can still find significant numbers of pure-blooded Indians. Chile has also been enriched by a sizable European immigration, especially German, Italian, Yugoslav, and Lebanese peoples.

Social structure in Chile is fairly well defined and there are a number of aristocratic families that trace their roots back to colonial days. There is an important and growing middle class composed of professionals. Their influence is felt in the political and economic life of the nation. Among the poor there is a large class known since the early days as the *rotos* or "broken ones." They are found mainly in the urban areas and live frequently in the shantytowns or *callampas* of the cities. Historians regard the valor of the *roto* as one of the major reasons for Chile's victory in the 1879 War of the Pacific.

Chile's holidays commemorate feast days of the Catholic Church or days related to important historical events such as Navy Day, on the 21st of May, and Chile's victory at the Battle of Iquique, and *Dia de la Raza.* The *Fiestas Patrias,* in mid-September, is a week-long celebration of national independence. It is during the holiday periods that one is able to observe the famous *cueca,* the most typical of Chilean folk dances. This dance expresses the courtship of a couple and the music is accompanied by the clapping of hands, stamping of heels, and waving of handkerchiefs.

Chile has a long and noble tradition in literature. The epic poem *La Araucana* is well-known to every school child. Chilean poets are world famous. Latin America's first Nobel Prize winner was a former rural school teacher, Gabriela Mistral. Mistral wrote poems of great love and tenderness and mastered a style that expressed emotion without being sentimental. Another Chilean Nobel Prize winner was the late Pablo Neruda. His poetry relied as much upon the reader's interpretations as the poet's intentions. In Chile today, there is a great encouragement for the arts, dance, and theatre. This reflects the country's continuing cultural tradition.

L. THE ECONOMY OF CHILE

To a large extent, Chile's economy is dependent upon its capacity to produce copper, nitrates, iron ore, and fishmeal. Chile has a large reserve of copper. Its ability to import other products is related to the price Chile receives for that mineral in the world markets. Chile is a classic example of an economy which is tied to one major crop or mineral resource. Chile relies on foreign imports of copper to gain income to maintain itself. In 1979, the total volume of copper produced exceeded one million tons.

Chile has sought to promote greater industrialization through the creation of the Chilean Development Corporation (CORFO). This group was established in 1939 to stimulate other areas of national production. In 1979, in an attempt to achieve greater development, Chile invested more than $370 million for hydroelectric, telecommunications, and iron and steel projects. Forestry is yet another industry which is increasing in importance due to the heavy foreign demand for quality wood. In 1979, Chile's commercial fishermen brought in a total of 2,250,00 tons of various sea products. Among other resources available in Chile are deposits of coal and a small reserve of petroleum which is not sufficient to meet the nation's long-term needs.

Chile has had a chronic problem of inflation. In 1973, the rate of inflation reached a peak of 400 percent. Since 1973, the military government has instituted measures to reduce public spending, returning over 400 companies to the private sector

Chile's diverse economy includes the largest surface copper mining operations in the world (top, left); cattle raising for export (top, right); and a growing steel industry (bottom).

from government control, and has invited foreign investments and credits. As a result of these measures and others, the sky-rocketing rate of inflation was brought to a manageable 38 percent in 1979. Critics of the government point out that inflation management was accomplished at a high social cost and that Chile continues to operate at a deficit in its international balance of payments.

M. THE OVERTHROW OF ALLENDE

In 1964, the Christian Democrats, led by Eduardo Frei, captured the presidency and promised the people of Chile a "Revolution in Liberty." The programs of Frei had not satisfied the dominant political parties in the country. In 1970, Dr. Salvador Allende, in his fourth try for the nation's highest office, gained a narrow victory over his conservative opponent and ex-president of the republic, Jorge Allesandri. Allende, as the head of a minority coalition of communists, socialists, and leftists, won support from the defeated Christian Democrats by agreeing to their demand to follow democratic and constitutional procedures once in office.

Allende was the first Marxist to be freely elected to head a nation in the Western Hemisphere. As president, he began a process of nationalizing the nation's mineral resources, and assumed control over the banks. Allende denounced the owners of the copper mines, many of them United States corporations. He also hinted that they could expect little in return because of their past "exploitations." The Allende government also ordered a 35 percent wage increase in early 1972, but enforced stiff price controls. There was an expansion in the money supply to pay the cost of increased public spending and inflation accelerated. In an attempt to satisfy his political followers, and to stimulate Chile's unproductive agricultural industry, the administration permitted the expropriation of 1,300 farms.

Discontent with the measures of the Allende government be-

161

came evident that same year as food shortages developed and housewives banging pots and pans paraded through the streets of the capital. At the same time, copper production declined as large numbers of technicians and other professionals left the country. Many defended the actions taken by the Allende government to transform the economy from a capitalistic to a socialist society. Others interpreted the protests by middle-class housewives and professionals as evidence that these groups could not accept the broader participation in political decision-making. However, popular discountent with Allede's policies grew.

By late 1972, Chile's economy had deteriorated badly. Foreign reserves declined to $100 million. Foreign investment and loans dried up. Strikes paralyzed a number of key industries. And armed clashes between supporters and defenders of the Allende government became common. These actions plus Chile's new opening of diplomatic relations with Communist countries caused unease in Chilean—U.S. relations. Relations between the two countries became embittered as Allende accused the United States of "strangling" Chile's economy and asked for assistance from the Soviet Union. Meanwhile, as technicians and experts from the Communist bloc nations, and especially Cuba, flocked to Chile, the inflation rate soared, reaching more than 300 percent in the first six months of 1973.

By June 1973, it became clear that the Chilean military would intervene. Strikes, runaway inflation, food shortages, and street fighting created pressures on the military to restore order as it had done in 1891. The justification here was the turbulent condition of the country, the allegation that Allende had subverted the constitution, and the interference in Chile's internal affairs by the several thousands of leftist exiles who had entered Chile. An abortive attempt at overthrowing the Allende government failed in June.

On September 11, 1973, the military acted with force and attacked the presidential palace. Salvador Allende died in the action and a military *junta* was installed under the leadership of army general Augusto Pinochet. The new government declared a state of siege and began arresting large numbers of Allende supporters. This was followed by allegations that the new military government was torturing and killing people in order to erase the Marxist influence from Chile. The military also disbanded political parties, prohibited labor strikes, and suspended civil liberties.

Since 1973, the *junta* in Chile has broken diplomatic relations with the Communist bloc nations. It has also returned many industries seized by the Allende government, and has directed the economy toward the free market. As a philosophical rationale for its actions, it has cited the need to strengthen and stabilize the country against all threats external and internal. In May 1980, President Pinochet declared that political activity, as it was known during the late 1960's and 1970's, would not be tolerated. The effect of such activity, he argued, was to divide the nation. To permit this he said, "would give Marxism another opportunity." Chile will return once again to civilian rule when "institutions are adopted that fit the social and cultural traditions of the people, and not through the adoption of those belonging to others."

QUESTIONS AND ACTIVITIES

KEY WORDS, PEOPLE, AND PHRASES

Can you identify and explain the following words, names, and phrases? Use an encyclopedia or dictionary if necessary.

Don Pedro II	*sertao*	Christian Democrats
Joao Goulart	Diego de Almagro	Eduardo Frei
Electoral College	Lautaro	Salvador Allende
favelas	Araucanian	exile

MULTIPLE CHOICE TEST

In each of the following, you have four answer choices. Choose the only correct answer.

1. On the east, Brazil bulges into *(a)* the Pacific Ocean, *(b)* the Atlantic Ocean, *(c)* the Caribbean Sea, *(d)* the Gulf of Mexico.
2. The capital city of Brazil is *(a)* Rio de Janeiro, *(b)* Belem, *(c)* Brasilia, *(d)* Montevideo.
3. The Brazilian government is like the United States government because both have *(a)* direct election of the president, *(b)* an elected judiciary, *(c)* separation of powers, *(d)* an appointed legislature.
4. The name of the government backed party in Brazil is *(a)* MAIPU, *(b)* ARENA, *(c)* MDB, *(d)* Christian Democrats.
5. The legislative branch of the Brazilian government consists of *(a)* Senate and House of Representatives, *(b)* House of Representatives and Chamber of Deputies, *(c)* Chamber of Deputies and Senate, *(d)* Senate and Parliament.
6. Which of the following helps account for Brazil's dwindling native Indian population? *(a)* intermarriage with Europeans, *(b)* deportation to other countries, *(c)* exposure to European diseases, *(d)* annihilation by white settlers.
7. The culture of Brazil could be said to be mainly *(a)* European, *(b)* Indian, *(c)* African, *(d)* mixed.
8. How many years will it take Brazil's population to double? *(a)* 200, *(b)* 25, *(c)* 100, *(d)* 50.
9. The large *favela* population of Rio de Janeiro is evidence of *(a)* poor city planning, *(b)* a population explosion, *(c)* the gap between rich and poor, *(d)* lack of agricultural work.
10. The countries located on Chile's eastern border are *(a)* Peru and Bolivia, *(b)* Uruguay and Bolivia, *(c)* Argentina and Bolivia, *(d)* Paraguay and Peru.
11. About which percentage of Chile's land is uninhabited? *(a)* 30 percent, *(b)* 45 percent, *(c)* 60 percent, *(d)* 75 percent.
12. Chile's first president and liberator from Spanish rule was *(a)* Lautaro, *(b)* O'Higgins, *(c)* Valdivia, *(d)* Almagro.
13. The 1879 War of the Pacific ended with Bolivia losing this port city to Chile: *(a)* Lima, *(b)* La Paz, *(c)* Valparaiso, *(d)* Antofagasta.

14. The Indians who stopped the advance of Spanish *conquistadores* in Chile were the *(a)* Araucanians, *(b)* Incas, *(c)* Aztecs, *(d)* Mayas.
15. The Chilean poet who was the first Latin American to win the Nobel Prize was *(a)* Huidobro, *(b)* Neruda, *(c)* Asturias, *(d)* Mistral.

THINGS TO DO

1. Prepare a report on the discovery of Brazil by Pedro Cabral.
2. Prepare a chart tracing the early rulers of Brazil. Include their accomplishments.
3. In a small group, prepare a report on the significance of the Carnival, the biggest Brazilian fiesta.
4. Draw a map of Brazil; use an atlas to locate its largest cities and major geographic features.
5. Research project: How is coffee grown, harvested, and exported by Brazil?
6. Prepare a report on the city of Brasília including its architecture, design, and the reasons for its creation.
7. Prepare a map on the various climate regions of Chile.
8. Present an oral report to your class on the Chilean *roto*, explain how he got his name, and relate his contributions to Chile's victory in the War of 1879.
9. Debate topic: Resolved—The present military junta saved Chile from the dangers of communism.
10. Research project: Discuss the role of the Central Intelligence Agency (C.I.A.) in the overthrow of Allende in Chile. Use *The New York Times Index* and the *Reader's Guide to Periodical Literature* to find articles on the C.I.A. in Chile.

9

LATIN AMERICA
AND THE WORLD

Any study of Latin America must take into account the variety of that region. The individual differences between the person who lives on the *altiplano* of Bolivia and the person living in Buenos Aires, the capital city of Argentina, are far greater than the differences between the citizen of Austria and someone living in the Netherlands. Some Latin American nations, such as Haiti, are among the poorest and least developed in the world. Others, such as Brazil, are among the leading nations of the world.

Thinking of the nations of Latin America as a block is not consistent with reality. As is true with all other nations, each country in Latin America frames a foreign policy it believes to be in its own best interests. What remains fundamental, however, is that each nation in Latin America must adopt a policy toward its neighbors, to the hemisphere, and to the world.

A. RELATIONS WITH THE UNITED STATES

United States policy makers often refer to the special relationship that exists between the United States and the nations of the Western Hemisphere. Mention is made of a common past as former colonies, of a shared European tradition, and a geographic proximity. The history of that special relationship shows that, from the point of view of the Latin Americans, the United States has more often acted the part of the "Colossus of the North" than "the Good Neighbor."

There has been no single United States policy toward Latin America. Nor has there been a series of policies that were an expression of the perceptions, times, and circumstances in which the policies were made. There are probably four time periods in which United States policy toward Latin America can be categorized: 1810 to 1895, 1896 to 1932, 1933 to 1945, and 1946 to the present.

1810 to 1895. During the early years of Latin America's independence movements, the United States, recently free from British domination, expressed sympathy and encouragement toward its fellow republics to the south. The United States was not able to do much more, since post-independence problems and another war with England in 1812 strained America's already limited resources. Following the defeat of Napoleon in 1814, there was a desire to restore European control over the new independent countries of Latin America. In 1823, in a message to the Congress, President James Monroe announced a policy that came to be known as the "Monroe Doctrine."

The Monroe Doctrine was a clear warning to Europe that the United States would not look with kindness on any attempt by Spain and Portugal to recover their former colonies. Citizens of the United States saw the new document as an expression of their country's concern with the well-being of its southern neighbors. In Latin America, however, the Monroe Doctrine was seen as an attempt by the United States to become the new master of the nations in the southern hemisphere.

Manifest Destiny. During the 1840's a new phrase entered the vocabulary of Americans which caused concern in Latin America. *Manifest Destiny* meant that the United States had an inevitable mission to expand its territory. American expansionists relied on this phrase to help justify the war with Mexico (1846-1848) and the acquisition of terriory resulting from that war. By the close of the 19th century, the United States had engaged in a number of episodes in support of the principles laid down in the Monroe Doctrine. Opposition to French intervention in Mexico, and Spanish attempts to re-annex the Dominican Republic were effected. Great Britain, in a dispute with Venezuela over boundary limits, was warned by the United States in 1895 that "... Today the United States is practically sovereign on this continent and its fiat is law upon the subjects to which it confines its interpositions."

1896 to 1932. The second stage of United States policy in Latin America was marked by a bold display of power. During this period the United States defeated Spain, annexed Puerto Rico, and secured a highly favorable treaty to win a naval base at Guantanamo Bay in Cuba. Through the Platt Amendment the United States reserved to its own determination the conditions for intervention in Cuban affairs. In 1903, the United States, in a thinly disguised move, provided the support necessary to gain Panama its independence from Colombia. In addition, the United States secured the right to build the new canal linking the Atlantic and Pacific Oceans.

In the years that followed construction of the Panama Canal, yet another phrase entered the vocabulary of inter-American relations—the Roosevelt Corollary. Under this new policy, the United States imposed varying degrees of control over a number of Latin American countries in the Caribbean and in Central America. Acting without fear of condemnation, the United States invaded Mexico twice. It was during this period that Latin

New York Sun

This cartoon shows Roosevelt moving the U.S. fleet around the Caribbean in his "Big Stick" application of the Monroe Doctrine.

Americans grew suspicious of United States motives in the hemisphere. The residue of bitterness continues to this day.

1933 to 1945. If the previous period was the low point of inter-American relations, the administration of President Franklin D. Roosevelt marked a welcome change. In truth, efforts to improve relations with Latin America had already begun in the Hoover Administration, but Roosevelt captured the imagination of the Latins with his Good Neighbor Policy. In a new departure, Roosevelt repudiated the Platt Amendment, ordered United States forces home from their bases in the Caribbean, and vowed to consult the nations of the hemisphere if the principles of the Monroe Doctrine were violated. A number of reciprocal trade agreements were signed and commerce between the United States and Latin America expanded greatly. In addition, a number of Pan-American conferences were arranged to improve communication and cooperation among the American republics. The fruits of these efforts were made evident during World War II, when the nations of the hemisphere, with a few exceptions, united behind Allied efforts to defeat the Axis powers.

1946 to Present. The war against the Axis had barely ended when a new period began to concern United States policy makers —the cold war. The cold war distracted concern with the Latin American republics and resulted in a new focus upon reconstruction in Europe, military defense, and meeting communist threats in eastern Europe and Asia. Latin America, at least until the middle 1950's, was regarded as safe from the threat of communism and was downgraded in United States foreign policy affairs. Until 1960, the United States foreign aid program in Latin America had reached a total of only two percent of the entire amount allocated in the budget for the purposes of helping poorer nations resist communism.

By 1954, threats to United States security caused the United States to take actions that created new unrest among the Latin American republics. Fear that a communist government was in the making in Guatemala led President Eisenhower to approve

CASE INQUIRY: The Good Neighbor Policy

Decades of strained relations between the United States and the nations of Latin America were reversed beginning with the Hoover Administration. A few years later, President Franklin Roosevelt, in a speech delivered in 1936, resolved to pursue a policy based on respect for Latin American affairs.

> In the field of world policy, I would dedicate this nation to the policy of the good neighbor—the neighbor who resolutely respects himself and, because he does so, respects the rights of others—the neighbor who respects his obligations and respects the sanctity of his agreements in and with a world of neighbors....
>
> The noblest monument to peace and to neighborly economic and social friendship in all the world is not a monument in bronze or stone, but the boundary which unites the United States and Canada—3,000 miles of friendship with no barbed wire, no gun or soldier, and no passport on the whole frontier. Mutual trust made that frontier. To extend the same sort of mutual trust throughout the Americans was our aim.
>
> The American republics to the south of us have been ready always to cooperate with the United States on a basis of equality and mutual respect, but before we inaugurated the good neighbor policy there was among them resentment and fear because certain administrations in Washington had slighted their national pride and their sovereign rights.
>
> We have negotiated a Pan American convention embodying the principle of nonintervention. We have abandoned the Platt Amendment, which gave us the right to intervene in the internal affairs of the Republic of Cuba. We have withdrawn American Marines from Haiti. We have signed a new treaty which places our relations with Panama on a mutually satisfactory basis. We have undertaken a series of trade agreements with other American countries to our mutual commercial profit. At the request of two neighboring republics, I hope to give assistance to the final settlement of the last serious boundary dispute between any of the American nations.

1. Why did the "Good Neighbor Policy" reflect a turning point in relations between the United States and Latin America?

2. What examples did President Roosevelt give of American intentions to be a "good neighbor?"

Peace and War: United States Foreign Policy 1931-1941. Washington, D.C. 1943. pp 323-329.

secret operations to overthrow the Arbenz government in that nation. Perhaps as an over-reaction to the prospect of communist infiltration, the United States began to give open support to Latin American dictators such as Batista, Trujillo, and Somoza. Americans were shocked when Vice-President Richard Nixon, in a good-will visit to Latin America in 1958, was cursed by angry and hostile crowds wherever he went.

In response to this deterioration in relations between the United States and the Latin American republics, President John F. Kennedy, in 1961, announced yet another policy. This was the Alliance for Progress. The thrust of the Alliance program was social, political, and economic reform in the Americas. As an underlying motive, there was the clear belief that these reforms would improve the lives of the Latin Americans and this in turn would prove the best deterrent to the spread of communism in the hemisphere.

The death of Kennedy and the failure of the Alliance programs to fulfill their expectations caused dismay in Latin America. When the United States sent Marines to intervene in the Dominican Republic in 1965, Latin Americans saw this as a repudiation of inter-American cooperation. President Lyndon Johnson argued that as much as he lamented the intervention, the danger of another Cuba left him with no alternative.

In the 1970's, the Nixon administration decided to abandon the social and economic aims of the Alliance for Progress. Instead Nixon called for a partnership between the United States and Latin America. President Nixon also made clear that the United States would not accept the seizure of property belonging to United States businesses in Latin America. During the Nixon years, the Central Intelligence Agency (C.I.A.) played a prominent role in Latin America, including financial aid to forces in Chile seeking to overthrow the government of Salvador Allende.

In the administration of President Jimmy Carter, the United States again pledged to work for reform and progress in Latin America. The cornerstone of the Carter policy was his program

In October 1979, Panama took over control of the former United States Canal Zone.

on human rights: a concern for individual civil, political, and economic freedoms as fundamental principles of life in the hemisphere. The new policy was aimed at those governments in Latin America who have taken repressive measures against their people, such as the imprisonment of people who disagree with government policies. For example, in Argentina, it was estimated that thousands of people disappeared in the government crackdown on political dissenters in the late 1970's.

B. INTER-AMERICAN RELATIONS

The unification of Latin America was the great dream of the liberator Simón Bolívar. Shortly before his death in 1830, he wrote: "America is ungovernable. Those who have served the revolution have plowed the sea." It was a thoughtful American statesman, James Blaine, who proposed a meeting of the nations of the Americas in Washington, D.C. in 1889. The aim of the meeting was to foster a sense of unity among the republics of the

Americas. Thus was created the Pan American Union, which lasted until 1948. After 1948 a new structure was composed, the Organization of American States (OAS). The purpose of the OAS was to provide mutual protection against aggression and the peaceful settlement of disputes among the American republics. A number of councils were also set up to further economic, cultural, and military cooperation. In the 1960's, collective action was taken against the dictators Trujillo in the Dominican Republic and Castro in Cuba. Many Latin Americans were reluctant to welcome OAS actions because they felt that the United States was using the machinery of the organization to accomplish American political purposes. The 1965 United States intervention in the Dominican Republic led directly to the 1967 Buenos Aires Protocol. This protocol effectively barred future collective action in the Americas. Over the past several years there have been attempts to establish a new organization for Latin American unity that would exclude the United States.

Port development is critically important for Latin American trade. The United Nations International Bank provided funds for the Port of Santos in Brazil.

United Nations

Boundary Conflicts. Some of the most difficult problems among the Latin American nations have revolved about the question of national boundaries. In South America, only Venezuela has never gone to war over a territorial dispute with a neighboring republic. Nevertheless, even Venezuela has been involved with serious problems regarding its territorial limits. The 1865 War of the Triple Alliance saw Brazil, Argentina, and Uruguay unite against solitary Paraguay. When the war ended four years later, the adult male population of all the countries involved was less than thirty thousand. In the War of the Pacific, which lasted from 1879 to 1883, Chile defeated the combined military forces of Peru and Bolivia. In the 1930's, Bolivia and Paraguay fought the Chaco War at a high cost of human lives. In 1940, Peru, which had long claimed a part of Ecuador's territory in the Amazon, bombed and invaded Ecuador.

In Central America, war broke out in 1906 among Guatemala, El Salvador, and Honduras. In 1969, the so called "Soccer War" was fought between El Salvador and Honduras over the migration of citizens of El Salvador into the territory of Honduras. In Guatemala today, the phrase "Colossus of the Noth" refers to Mexico's territorial ambitions as much as to the United States. In addition, there have been a number of continuing disputes between Panama and Costa Rica, Costa Rica versus Nicaragua, and so on.

In the Caribbean, territorial wars and the added dimension of racial tensions have influenced relations between the Dominican Republic and Haiti. In 1980, Cuba, which has made an effort to win the goodwill of the black nations in the region, sent its aircraft against Bahamian fishing boats for allegedly violating Cuban territorial waters. Cuba's position in the Socialist camp and its attempts to export revolution has angered a number of Latin American governments.

In Search of Unity. Despite important differences, there is hope for unity and cooperation among the various Latin American republics. Agreement has been reached on broad policy issues such as a respect for non-intervention, the acceptance of 200 miles as the off-shore water limits, the right of political asylum, and the use of arbitration to resolve disputes. For example, in 1980, Chile and Argentina averted war by submitting a territorial question to the Vatican in Rome. In that same year, Argentina and Brazil signed a number of formal agreements designed to better integrate their efforts toward mutual benefit.

In the area of economic activity, a number of steps have been taken to enlarge markets and increase the standard of living of the people in the region. Included among these regional groupings are:

1. The Latin American Free Trade Association (LAFTA)
2. The Andean Group
3. The Central American Common Market (CACM)
4. The Caribbean Free Trade Association (CARIFTA)

Repeated efforts to merge the regional associations into a Latin American Common Market have been unsuccessful.

C. WORLD RELATIONS

Latin America has had a high regard for Europe and its institutions. From the days of independence, Latin Americans imitated European styles, culture, and architecture. In order to reduce dependence upon the United States, Latin Americans have tried to diversify their markets and sources of supply. They have not, however, been as successful as they would like. This lack of success is due in part to the European Common Market, which aims to foster trade among its member nations. Even Latin America's traditional trading partner, Great Britain, has diverted its trade from Latin America to the European mainland. Consequently, the chances for expanded trade between Latin America and the European continent are not good. Japan, on the other hand, has increased its trade with Latin America enormously over the past decade. For example, Argentina exports to Japan in 1965 amounted to $32.4 million. In 1974, the export figures were more than $135 million. Chile's exports to Japan in 1965 were only $74 million by 1974, the figure reached $407 million. In Japan, the Latin Americans have found a trading partner that needs their abundant primary resources. In Latin America, Japan has found another growing market for its manufactured goods.

Latin American countries as a whole are far more advanced industrially than any of the Third World countries. Furthermore, the issues that concern the other less developed countries, such as control over foreign investment, are no longer major problems in Latin America. In calling for a new economic order, Latin Americans provide the intellectual leadership for other Third World nations. There is some question, however, as to the Latin American demand for a fairer distribution of the world's resources when the elites that govern the Latin American nations are reluctant to impose the same upon themselves.

QUESTIONS AND ACTIVITIES

KEY WORDS, PEOPLE, AND PHRASES

Can you identify and explain the following words, names and phrases? Use an encyclopedia or dictionary if necessary.

altiplano	Alliance for Progress	Franklin D. Roosevelt
Monroe Doctrine	"The Soccer War"	James Blaine
Manifest Destiny	Chaco War	John F. Kennedy
Andean Group	cold war	"Colossus of the North"
Platt Amendment	Lyndon Johnson	War of the Triple Alliance
human rights	Roosevelt Corollary	Good Neighbor Policy

MULTIPLE CHOICE TEST

In each of the following, you have four answer choices. Choose the only correct answer.

1. Which Latin American nation is a good prospect to emerge as a leading power among nations? *(a)* Chile, *(b)* Cuba, *(c)* Brazil, *(d)* Peru.

2. In general, United States foreign policy toward Latin America has been *(a)* friendly, *(b)* aggressive, *(c)* indifferent, *(d)* inconsistent.

3. The 1840's United States policy to expand to the Pacific Coast was called *(a)* the Monroe Doctrine, *(b)* Manifest Destiny, *(c)* Dollar Diplomacy, *(d)* the Good Neighbor Policy.

4. The Roosevelt Corollary was a United States policy to keep a tight control over *(a)* South America, *(b)* the Caribbean and Central America, *(c)* the Pacific Ocean, *(d)* the North Sea.

5. The United States president identified with the Good Neighbor Policy is *(a)* Harry Truman *(b)* Franklin D. Roosevelt, *(c)* Theodore Roosevelt, *(d)* John F. Kennedy.

6. The purpose for the creation of the Pan American conferences was to *(a)* settle the War of the Pacific, *(b)* give foreign aid to Haiti, *(c)* improve relations among the countries of the Americas, *(d)* help protect United States business interests in Latin America.

7. The fear of communism caused President Eisenhower to intervene in the politics of *(a)* Chile, *(b)* Guatemala, *(c)* Puerto Rico, *(d)* Peru.

8. To meet the challenge to the hemisphere posed by Fidel Castro, John F. Kennedy proposed the *(a)* Platt Amendment, *(b)* Alliance for Progress, *(c)* Marshall Plan, *(d)* Food for Peace Programs.

9. Which of these leaders of Latin American nations was not a dictator? *(a)* Batista, *(b)* Frei, *(c)* Trujillo, *(d)* Somoza.

10. Fear of another Cuba caused this United States President to send troops into the Dominican Republic. *(a)* Kennedy, *(b)* Johnson, *(c)* Nixon, *(d)* Ford.

11. A concern for the individual's personal liberties is part of President Carter's program of *(a)* human rights, *(b)* watchful waiting, *(c)* "partners of the Americas," *(d)* New Deal.

12. The only South American nation that has never gone to war over a territorial dispute is *(a)* Brazil, *(b)* Colombia, *(c)* Paraguay, *(d)* Venezuela.
13. Which of these nations does *not* belong to the Andean Group? *(a)* Peru, *(b)* Bolivia, *(c)* Ecuador, *(d)* Argentina.
14. Which nation would *not* belong to the Caribbean Free Trade Association? *(a)* the Dominican Republic, *(b)* Jamaica, *(c)* Bahamas, *(d)* Uruguay.
15. An Asian nation that is making important inroads in developing trade relations in Latin America is *(a)* China, *(b)* India, *(c)* Japan, *(d)* Vietnam.

THINGS TO DO

1. Investigate the history of United States intervention in Latin America. Give the dates of intervention, reasons for, and outcome of each incident.
2. Read a profile of James Blaine. Why was he interested in acting to improve relations with Latin America? In an oral report to your class tell why you think he was a man ahead of his times.
3. Prepare a report on the Latin American attempts to form agreements to integrate their economies. Be sure you include the problems involved in making agreements and the prospects for success.
4. Idea for debate: Resolved—Before Latin America can unite as a political unit it must first succeed in establishing satisfactory economic agreements.
5. Draw a time line of important dates regarding United States policy in Latin America.

10

ECONOMIC, POLITICAL, AND SOCIAL CHANGE IN LATIN AMERICA

Latin America is a region in a state of continuous and rapid change. Because of the enormous size of Latin America, its diversity of peoples, cultures, and national organization, understanding its complexity is not easy. Nevertheless, there are developing trends that deserve attention in order to learn where Latin America is heading in the last two decades of the 20th century.

A.   ECONOMIC CHANGE

Since 1960, the fastest growing sector in the economy of Latin America has been industry. Industrialization appears to be the fastest way to bring about modernization, increased employment for a rising population, and the long sought after goal of improved income distribution. There is no question that Latin America's greatest challenge in the 1980's is finding employment for its population. With an annual increase of 2.9 percent, Latin America is the world leader in population growth.

The rapid growth of population and the marked shift of people from rural areas to large urban centers is happening so fast that the national economies of countries cannot absorb them.

The reasons for the shift from rural regions to the cities of Latin America are not difficult to understand. The attractions and apparent opportunities of big city life far outweigh life in the farming areas. Education for one's children is another incentive for urban migration. Most rural workers are functionally illiterate and lack marketable skills, and so they are unemployable. They are forced to live on the fringe of urban life in shantytowns and slums that are found in every major city in Latin America. In response, the governments in the region are attempting to

The communication revolution has reached nearly all Latin American cities. Television antennas top the roofs of the working class poor in Buenos Aires, Argentina.

provide jobs by investing in heavy industry projects such as steel production and automobile factories. To conserve currency reserves, governments are relying on a program of import substitution. Such program will provide employment and develop local industry. Yet another hope for improvement is "importing" knowledge and technology from the advanced countries of the world. Access to such information will make it easier for Latin American nations to market their goods world wide. There is also the need for greater capital investments from the developed countries.

Some economists question whether the attainment of these goals of modernization, substitution, technology, and foreign investment will really contribute to providing employment for Latin America's rapidly growing population. Critics of these measures point out that the attainment of these goals will only add to greater unemployment! They argue that improvement in all of these areas will result in more efficient and labor saving techniques, thus resulting in less employment, and not more.

Foreign assistance in the form of aid and investments appear less welcome to many Latin Americans. They fear the high costs of repayment with interest or the political consequences of external control, or domination which often accompanies invest- ments from abroad. It would seem therefore that Latin America's greatest task in the remaining two decades of this century is to either control population growth or stimulate internal develop- ment to provide more jobs, and to devise new strategies for train- ing young people entering the work force.

B.   POLITICAL CHANGE

It is now more than twenty years since the Cuban revolution, and despite all of the vigor and rhetoric, no country in Latin America is following the Cuban model for political change. There are a number of reasons offered to explain the failure of the revolution to spread throughout the hemisphere. Some of these include the belief that the revolution has "sold out" by imposing an alien ideology, Marxism, on its nationalistic thrust and by being too close to the political line set down by the Soviet Union. The nationalist-minded Latin American revolutionaries are not prepared to trade dependency and subordination of their interests from one alien world power, the United States, to another, the Soviet Union.

On the other hand, North Americans studying Latin American political systems and governments over the years have often found fault with the apparent defects and deficiencies of those governments and their lack of democratic practices. If one is to understand Latin America, one must keep in mind that the cul- tural base from which the political system springs is not demo- cratic in the Anglo-American tradition. Indeed, there is ample evidence to suggest that much of the chronic instability that has characterized government in Latin America may be traced to the attempts to borrow formulas from other nations with different historical experiences and adapt them to local conditions. Since these political concepts and ideals were foreign and without national foundations, subverting them never proved difficult by the decision-makers in power.

In the traditional Latin America of yesterday, participation in the political life of the nation was reserved to a small portion of

Writing political slogans on walls is an old custom in Latin America. This one in Lima, Peru, says "only the revolution will give the people bread, liberty, and education. Let us follow the example of Che (Guevera)."

the population. These were the people who enjoyed the benefits of education, wealth, and social status. These *elites*, as they were called, usually ruled as one part of a coalition, with the Church and the military. Each of the elements acted together to support the system. As a result of the weaknesses of an undeveloped democratic political system, military participation and authority in times of crisis became sanctioned in a number of Latin American countries by constitutional law.

However, the dynamics of change have affected these "pillars" of the old established order and will probably shape military actions in the future. In much of Latin America the traditional landowning oligarchy is giving way to a new and steadily developing professional/managerial elite. This new class has little interest in maintaining the privileges of the old order. The Church itself has become the leading agent for reform and improvement.

Furthermore, as Latin America continues in its transition from a traditional to a modern society, the changes resulting from population growth and shifts will impact upon the political system. The migration pattern from the rural areas to the urban areas is bound to set off a number of consequences. These include a demand for public services including schools, hospitals, and housing. Exposure to communication media and the increase of literacy will inevitably affect participation in the political process.

C. SOCIAL CHANGE

Change takes place along three broad fronts: economic, political, and social. The important clues to observe in Latin America in the coming years is how the various social structures deal with the challenges presented by a large population increase and heavy migration from the rural areas to the cities. It is estimated that at the end of 1980, the share of the population living in the urban areas increased from 39 percent in 1950 to almost 61 percent. Experts in the field of social relations are not in agreement over the effects of this mass movement. Some see in this change a positive sign. Because with all of its defects, life in the city still offers better hopes for the migrant than does life in the rural areas. They also point out that migration usually involves shifts, not of individuals or couples, but entire groups of families, relatives and close friends. In such a setting, with security provided by the closeness of familiar persons, the adjustment and transition from rural life to urban life is made easier. Other experts do not share this view. They express concern about the concentration of so many people from different backgrounds living close together in conditions of poverty. As awareness of inequality develops, experts claim that life in the urban areas will be marked by conflict between social classes, labor unrest, and class-oriented politics. Socioligists who hold this view believe that unless immediate action is taken by the decision-makers in Latin America to face these problems, prospects for social harmony are not good. Part of the problem is how to deal with the problems. There is agreement that income distribution is good measurement of a nation's social organization, yet the methods for achieving redistribution of wealth, income, and resources in Latin America without resort to revolution and violence is a goal yet to be achieved.

Other social trends to watch in the next ten years are the extent to which the traditional values and customs of Latin Americans undergo change as a result of their exposure to the mass media, especially television. Imported movies and talk shows inform many Latin Americans about life in other parts of the world. There is no doubt that the modern European and North American culture and standard of living is affecting the way Latin Americans think and act. In every major city one can hear the latest music and see a Hollywood film and eat hamburgers and french fries in fast food restaurants. In addition, there are signs that women in Latin America no longer wish to accept a secondary status in society. Latin American feminists are demanding equal rights and equal opportunities like their sisters in Western nations.

The Third World nations are the developing countries in Asia, Africa, and Latin America. It is generally agreed that as a bloc the Latin American nations are the more developed and industrialized. The entire world, including the developed nations, will be watching Latin America closely to see how the economic, political, and social problems are solved.

Daniel J. Mugan

Although the architecture of the Church in Latin America shows the European influence, recent efforts by church leaders have championed the needs of the poor, particularly the native Indians and mestizos.

QUESTIONS AND ACTIVITIES

KEY WORDS AND PHRASES

Can you explain the meaning of the following words or phrases? Use a dictionary or encyclopedia if necessary.

stereotype
exchange currency
rural region
urban region
shantytown
import substitution

transfer of knowledge
nationalism
migrants
Anglo-American tradition
patterns of migration
decision-makers

MULTIPLE CHOICE TEST

In each of the following you have four possible answer choices. Select the only correct answer.

1. The fastest growing sector of the economy in Latin America is *(a)* agricultural, *(b)* service, *(c)* industrial, *(d)* government.
2. Latin America's traditional way of earning currency exchange is through *(a)* arms sales, *(b)* mining and agriculture, *(c)* manufacturing, *(d)* service industries.
3. The approximate per annual rate of population growth in Latin America is *(a)* 1 percent, *(b)* 3 percent, *(c)* 8 percent, *(d)* 61 percent.
4. The rate of migration from farms to cities throughout Latin America is at a pace best described as *(a)* slow, *(b)* moderate, *(c)* fast, *(d)* none of these.
5. Examples of capital industries are *(a)* steel works, *(b)* handcrafts, *(c)* chains of supermarkets, *(d)* tourism.
6. Which of the following is considered Latin America's greatest problem in the near future? *(a)* literacy programs, *(b)* employment, *(c)* running out of natural resources, *(d)* urbanization.
7. Failure to devise institutions to replace those of Spanish colonialism is frequently reflected in Latin America's *(a)* religious, *(b)* political, *(c)* social, *(d)* economic institutions.
8. In the Latin America of yesterday, voting in elections was generally *(a)* widespread, *(b)* restricted, *(c)* eliminated, *(d)* encouraged.

185

9. The "Establishment" in Latin America was by tradition composed of *(a)* landowners, Church, and military, *(b)* Liberals, peasants, and workers, *(c)* military, Church, and farm workers, *(d)* landowners, Conservatives, and military.
10. Generally, one can expect the military in future Latin American politics to play a role best described as *(a)* non-involved, *(b)* active, *(c)* supportive, *(d)* cautious.
11. Which is a common reason for moving to the city from the country side? *(a)* the ability to use public transportation, *(b)* chance to see and be with a higher class of people, *(c)* opportunity to earn a better living, *(d)* escape the problems of pollution.
12. Experts who study how groups and classes of people relate to each other are known as *(a)* historians, *(b)* sociologists, *(c)* physicians, *(d)* anthropologists.
13. Income distribution is a question that usually interests *(a)* sociologists, *(b)* economists, *(c)* historians, *(d)* anthropologists.
14. Which of the following should not be classified as a "Third World" nation? *(a)* Haiti, *(b)* India, *(c)* Sudan, *(d)* Canada.

THINGS TO DO

1. Prepare a scrapbook of newspaper clippings about Latin America. Divide the book into three sections: economic, political, and social news.
2. Form a committee with two other members of your class and let each person discuss a topic related to the economic, political, and social affairs of a Latin American country.
3. Research project: The impact of rural migration upon Latin America's urban development.
4. Idea for a debate: Resolved—That Latin America examine the existing social, economic, and political systems in the world such as capitalism, socialism, etc., and adapt the one most likely to prove successful.
5. Prepare a report on how the United States can best help Latin America solve its problems.
6. Write a letter to a Latin American embassy or consulate and find out how that particular country is attempting to deal with its development problems.
7. Draw a chart showing the various rates of population growth in Latin America.

SELECTED BIBLIOGRAPHY

Alexander, Robert Jackson. *Today's Latin America,* 2nd ed. New York, Praeger, 1968.

Allende, Salvador. *Chile's Road to Socialism.* Baltimore, Penguin, 1973.

Asturias, Miguel Angel. *The President.* Baltimore, Penguin, 1972.

Baily, Samuel, ed. *Nationalism in Latin America.* New York, Knopf, 1970.

Beals, Carleton. *Nomads and Empire Builders: Native Peoples and Cultures of South America.* New York, Citadel Press, 1965.

Bernal, Ignacio. *Mexico before Cortez.* Garden City, Anchor, 1975.

Burland, Cottie A. *Peru Under the Incas.* New York, Putnam, 1967.

Bushnell, David, ed. *The Liberator: Simon Bolivar.* New York, Knopf, 1970.

Chapman, Walker. *The Golden Dream: Seekers of El Dorado.* Indianapolis, Bobbs-Merrill, 1967.

Chisley, Donald Barr. *The Spanish American Wars.* New York, Crown Publishers, 1971.

Clissold, Stephen. *Latin America: New World, Third World.* New York, Praeger, 1972.

Collier, John. *Indians of the Americas.* Abridged ed. New York, New American Library, 1948.

Diaz del Castillo, Bernal. *The Conquest of New Spain.* Translated with an intro. by J. M. Cohen. Baltimore, Penguin Books, 1963.

Ediger, Donald. *The Well of Sacrifice.* New York, Doubleday, 1971.

Fitzpatrick, Joseph P. *Puerto Rican Americans: The Meaning of Migration to the Motherland.* Englewood Cliffs, New Jersey, Prentice-Hall, 1971.

Friedrich, Paul. *Agrarian Revolt in a Mexican Village.* Englewood Cliffs, New Jersey, Prentice-Hall, 1970.

Goodsell, James Nelson. *Fidel Castro's Personal Revolution in Cuba.* New York, Knopf, 1975.

Gorz, Andre. *Socialism and Revolution.* Garden City, Anchor, 1973.

Greenleaf, Richard E., ed. *The Roman Catholic Church in Colonial America.* New York, Knopf, 1971.

Hahner, June, E. *Women in Latin American History.* Los Angeles, University of California at Los Angeles Press, 1976.

Hardoy, Jorge, ed. *Urbanization in Latin America.* Garden City, Anchor, 1975.

Kinsbrunner, Jay. *Chile: A Historical Interpretation.* New York, Harper, 1973.

Lawrence, David H. *The Plumed Serpent; Quetzalcoatl.* Intro. by William York Tindall. New York, Random House, 1955.

Llosa, Mario Vargas. *The Green House.* New York, Bard, 1973.

Marquez, Gabriel Garcia. *One Hundred Years of Soltitude.* New York, Avon, 1972.

Nelson, Lowry. *Cuba: The Measure of a Revolution.* Minneapolis, University of Minneapolis Press, 1972.

Nuñez Cabeza de Vaca, Alvar. *Adventures in the Unknown Interior of America.* New York, Collier Books, 1972.

Pescatello, Ann M., ed. *The African in Latin America.* New York, Knopf, 1975.

Powell, Jane P. *Ancient Art of the Americas.* Brooklyn, Brooklyn Museum, 1959.

Prescott, William A. *The World of the Incas.* Geneva, Minerva, 1970.

Rivera, Julius. *Latin America: A Sociocultural Interpretation.* New York, Appleton-Century Crofts, 1971.

Sexton, Patricia Cayo. *Spanish Harlem: Anatomy of Poverty.* New York, Harper and Row, 1965.

Tannenbaum, Frank. *Ten Keys to Latin America.* New York, Random House, 1966.

Von Hagen, Victor W. *The Aztec: Man and Tribe.* New York, New American Library, 1958.

_____*Realm of the Incas.* New York, New American Library, 1957.

_____*World of the Maya.* New York, New American Library, 1960.

Wagenheim, Karl and Olga. *The Puerto Ricans: A Documentary History.* Garden City, Anchor, 1973.

Wagley, Charles. *An Introduction to Brazil.* New York, Columbia University Press, 1971.

Wauchope, Robert, ed. *The Indian Background in Latin American History.* New York, Knopf, 1971.

Woodward, Ralph Lee Jr. *Central America: A Nation Divided.* New York, Oxford University Press, 1976.

Yanez, Augustin. *The Edge of the Storm.* Austin, University of Texas Press, 1971.

GLOSSARY

Altiplano: A high plateau, such as the one found in Bolivia.

Audiencia: The highest court in Spanish colonial America.

Barrio: A section of the city or neighborhood where the poor or working class live.

Cabildo: The municipal council in colonial Spanish America.

Caudillo: A strong or powerful leader.

Criollo: A white person born in America of Spanish parentage during colonial times.

Cruzeiro: Brazilian unit of currency.

Ejido: Community-owned lands in Mexico.

Encomienda: A grant or fief given by the king for loyal services.

Estancia: A large tract of land or estate in Argentina.

Favela: A squatter settlement in Brazilian cities.

Gaucho: An Argentine cowboy

Golpe De Estado: The military overthrow of a government.

Hacienda: A large estate in Spanish America, especially in Mexico.

Inquilino: A tenant farmer in Chile.

Junta: A board or ruling group.

Latifundia: Large landed estate in Spanish America which was usually not cultivated.

Mazombo: A white person born in America of Portuguese parentage during colonial times.

Mestizo: A person born of white and Indian parents.

Obrero: A worker in a factory.

Peninsular: A white person born in Europe who came to settle in Spanish colonial America.

Peón: A field laborer.

Peso: A monetary unit used in many Latin American countries.

Pueblo: A town or people.

Reinol: A white person born in Europe who settled in colonial Brazil.

Roto: A Chilean field laborer.

Sambo: A person of mixed Indian and black parentage.

Serape: Indian outergarment worn in Mexico.

Sertão: The interior or backlands of Brazil.

Trabajadores: Workers.

Tribunal: Court of Justice.

Vaqueros: Cowboys or herdsmen.

Yerba Mate: Popular tea beverage in Argentina, Paraguay, and Uruguay.

Index

Acapulco, Mexico, 80, 96

agriculture, 11, 20-24; Aztecs, 35; in Brazil, 11, 142, 151-152; cash crops, 130; in Central America, 21, 22, 127; in Chile, 161; in Costa Rica, 129-130; in Cuba, 101-103; Incas, 37, 38; Mayas, 33; in Mexico, 84, 93-94; in Nicaragua, 132; in Puerto Rico, 115, 121; reform, 24-25; subsistence farming, 26; in South America, 22; in the West Indies, 20-21

Alemán, Miguel, 84

Alexander VI, Pope, 40, 65

Allende, Salvador, 156, 161-163, 171

Allesandri, Jorge, 161

Alliance for Progress, 149, 171

Almagro, Diego de, 155

Almerda, Amenco de, 69

alpacas, 20

altiplano, 166

Amazon Basin, 12-13, 139, 140, 145; climate, 19

Amazon River, 7-8, 12; tributaries, 7

Andes Mountains, 5, 8, 9, 10, 12, 14, 20, 139, 154, 155

Andrada e Silva, José Bonifacio, 142

animals, 12, 13

Arawak (Indians), 115

architecture, 1, 71; of Brazil, 71; Incan, 31, 37; Mayan, 32; of Mexico, 89

Argentina, 2, 4, 5, 8, 10, 139, 145, 172; agriculture, 11; minerals, 26

Art, 70-71; Aztec, 31, 36; Mayan, 31, 34; Mexican, 89

Arucanian (Indians), 155, 158

Asturias, Miguel Angel, 69

Atacama Desert, 20, 154

Atahualpa, 39

Auraucanian (Indians), 30

Aztecs, 30, 34-36, 41, 67, 80, 155; agriculture, 35; art, 36; center of civilization, 35-36; decline, 41

Bahama Islands, location, 2

Baja California, 2, 17, 79

Balboa, Vasco Nuñez de, 40

Balmaceda, President, 156

bananas, 21-22, 93, 103, 127, 129, 130

Batista, Fulgencio, 105, 171

Bay of Pigs incident, 109

Belém, Brazil, 13, 150

Belize, 2, 18, 126

Belo Horizonte, Brazil, 150

Bingham, Hiram, 37

Bío-Bío River, 155, 158

blacks, 46, 59, 130, 132, 143, 146

Blaine, James, 172

Bolívar, Simón, 48, 49, 172

Bolivia, 2, 5, 7, 8, 11, 110, 139, 156; agriculture, 24; minerals, 26

Bonaparte, Joseph, 47

Borges, Jorge Luis, 69

boundary conflicts, 173-174

Brasília, Brazil, 13, 71, 149

Brazil, 1, 4, 7, 8, 13, 139-154, 166; agriculture, 11, 142, 151-152; architecture, 71; art, 70; cities, 11, 149-151; climate, 140; colonialism, 44, 140-142; culture, 59, 146; economy, 151-153; education, 142, 146-147; foods, 74; government, 143-145, 147, 148; health, 147-148; history, 140-143; housing, 147-148; independence, 50, 141; Indians, 145; industry, 142, 152-153; language, 140; literature, 69; location, 139; natural resources, 24, 26, 151, 152, 153-154; population, 139, 145, 147; religion, 146; social progress, 146; tourism, 150; topography, 139-140; trade, 142, 152, 154; transportation, 142; the U.S. and, 151

Brazilian Highlands, 11, 12, 140; climate, 19
Brooke, John R., 116
Bryan-Chamorro Treaty, 133
Buenos Aires, Argentina, 3, 7, 8, 69, 75
Buenos Aires Protocol, 172
bullfighting, 75
burros, 10

cabildos (town councils), 50
Cabral, Pedro Alvares, 140
cacao, 22, 73, 101, 129, 152
Calles, Plutarco Elías, 84
Camacho, Manuel Avila, 84
captaincies, 140
Carazo, Rodrigo, 130
Cárdenas, Lázaro, 84
carnival, 146
Campo Grande, Brazil, 12
Cape Horn, 2, 4
Caribbean America, 1, 2, 100-122, 173; minerals, 26
Carib (Indians), 30
carnauba wax, 13
Carranza, Venustiano, 83
Carter, Jimmy, 171
Casas, Bartolomé de las, 67
cash crops, 130
Castro, Fidel, 106-112, 172
Catholicism, 1, 64, 88, 120, 146, 158
cattle, 13, 103, 132
caudillo, 52-53, 67, 112
Central America, 5, 126-136, 173; agriculture, 21-22, 127; climate 18; location 1, 126; *map*, 126; topography, 127
Central American Common Market (CACM), 131
Central Intelligence Agency (C.I.A.), 109, 110, 171
Céspedes, Carlos Manuel de, 104
Chacabuco, Chile, 155
Chaco War (1930s), 173
Chalapa, Lake, 95

Chibcha (Indians), 30
Chile, 2, 14, 139, 154-163, 171; agriculture, 161; climate, 18, 154; colonialism, 67, 155; culture, 158-159; economy, 156, 159-161, 162; government, 156, 161-163; history, 155-158, human rights, 163, independence, 52, 155, 158; industry, 159-161; inflation, 159, 161, 162; *junta,* 162-163; literature, 158, military, 162-163; minerals, 20, 25, 156, 161; people, 158; population, 154; relations with Latin American nations, 156; social structure, 158; topography, 154; trade, 159; the U.S. and, 156, 161, 162; the U.S.S.R. and, 162, 163; War of the Pacific (1879), 156, 158
Chilean Development Corporation (CORFO), 159
Church: architecture, 71; in Mexico, 84, 88; power of the, 52, 82, 182
Churriguera, José de, 89
Ciboneys (Indians), 101
Ciudad Bolivar, Venezuela, 8
Clayton-Bulwar Treaty, 132
climate, 5, 14-20; in Brazil, 140; in Central America, 18; in Chile, 18, 154; in Costa Rica, 129; in Mexico, 17-18, 80; in South America, 18-20; vertical, definition, 14, 17-18; in the West Indies, 15-17
coffee, 19, 21, 92-93, 115, 121, 127, 129, 130, 132, 139, 151
cold war, 169
Colombia, 7, 8, 13, 126, 139; agriculture, 24; minerals, 26
Colonial period, 44-48; in Brazil, 140-142; in Chile, 67, 155; in Cuba, 103-104; law, 59; in Mexico, 81-82; in Puerto Rico, 115-116
colono system, 102
Colorado River, 10
Columbus, Christopher, 30, 34, 40, 67, 103, 115, 129, 132

communications, 10, 151, 159, 182, 184
Communism, Cuba and, 107-112
composers (music), 75
conquistadores, 40-41, 58, 64, 67, 129, 155
copper, 20, 156, 159, 162
Cordoba, Francisco Hernández de, 81, 132
Coronado, Francisco, 41
Cortázar, Julio, 69
Cortés, Hernán, 36, 41, 67, 81, 96, 103, 155
Cortines, Adolfo Ruiz, 84
Costa, Lucio, 151
Costa Rica, 2, 18, 126, 127, 129-131; agriculture, 22, 129-130; climate, 129; education, 130; government, 129, 131; history, 129-130; Indians in, 129, 130; minerals, 26; population, 130; typography, 129; transportation, 129
criollos, 46, 47, 49
Cuba, 2, 99-112, 127, 130, 171, 172; agriculture, 21, 101-103; Bay of Pigs incident, 109; communism, 107-112; economy, 105, 111, 112; health, 104; history, 105-111; government, 105, 106, 108-110; independence, 104; *map,* 100; minerals, 103, 105; Missile Crisis, 110; mountains, 100; natural resources, 103; relations with Latin America, 110, 136; revolution, 106-112, 181; Spanish American War, 104; Soviet relations, 107, 109, 111; topography, 100-101; the U.S. and, 104-105, 107, 109, 110, 111
Cuernavaca, Mexico, 96
Cuiaba River, 12
culture, 58-75, 146; art and architecture, 70-71, 89- 91; in Chile, 158; customs, 60-61; dress, family life, 72-74; foods, 73, 74; housing, 73; language, 59-60; literature, 67-69;

marriage, 72; in Mexico, 88-93; music and dancing, 74, 75; religion, 64-66; sports, 75
Curaçao, 2
customs, 60-61, 72-74; dating, 72; god-parents, 72; marriage, 72-73; in Mexico, 88
Cuzco, 37

da Gama, Vasco, 40
dancing, 74-75
Dario, Ruben, 68
de Soto, Hernando, 41
Dessalines, Jean-Jacques, 48
Díaz, Bartholomew, 40
Díaz, Porfirio, 83
Dominican Republic, 2, 167, 171, 172; agriculture, 21
dress, 74
Dutch, in the New World, 141

earthquakes, 127
Easter Island, 154
Echeverría Alvarez, Luis, 84, 86
economic change in Latin America, 179-181
economy: in Brazil, 151-153; in Chile, 156, 159-161, 162; in Cuba, 105, 111, 112; in Mexico, 84, 92-97; in Puerto Rico, 117, 121
Ecuador, 2, 5, 7, 139; foods, 74; minerals, 26
education, 62-63, 179; in Brazil, 142, 146-147; in Costa Rica, 130; in Puerto Rico, 116, 122; secondary schools, 63
Eisenhower, Dwight D., 169
ejidos, 24, 84, 93, 94
El Morro (fortress), 114, 115
El Salvador, 2, 18, 126, 127, 136; minerals, 26
employment, 179, 180
encomienda, 24
Ercillay, Zúñiga, Alonso de, 67
estancias, 24
estuaries, definition, 8

exploration of the New World, 30, 58, 101, 115, 129, 140

Mexico City, 69, 80, 81, 82, 84, 95, 97
military, power of, 52-53, 127, 144, 162-163, 181
Minas Gerais, 141
mineral resources, 11, 25-27, 132, 139; 151, 152, 153-154, 156, 161; chart 26
missionaries, 52-64
Missle Crisis, Cuban, 110
Mistral, Gabriela, 69, 158-159
Moncado, President, 133
Monroe, James, 167
Monroe Doctrine, 167, 169
Monterrey, Mexico, 18, 80
Montevideo, Uruguay, 8
Montezuma I, 35
Montezuma II, 36, 41, 81
Morelos, José María, 49, 82
mountains, 5-7, 9, 10; in Central America, 127; in Cuba, 100
Movimiento Pro-Independencia (MPI), 119
mulattoes, 47, 58, 101
Muñoz Marin, Luis, 117, 118, 120, 121

Napoleon, 47, 50, 142, 167
Napoleon III, 83
Neruda, Pablo, 69, 159
New World, discovery and exploration, 30-41
Nicaragua, 2, 18, 126, 127, 131-136; agriculture, 132; canal plan, 132, 133; Cuban relations, 136; government, 135-136; history, 132-135; Indians in, 132; minerals, 26, 132; population, 132; revolution, 135-136; *Sandinistas,* 135-136; topography, 131; the U.S. and, 133; 135, 136
Nicaragua, Lake, 131
Niemeyer, Oscar, 71, 150
Nixon, Richard, 171

Obregón, Alvaro, 83, 84
O'Gorman, Juan, 70

O'Higgins, Bernardo, 49, 155
oil, 84; in Mexico, 86, 87, 94, 97-98
oligarchy, 52, 182
"Operation Bootstrap," 117, 121-122
Ordaz, Gustavo Díaz, 84
Organization of American States (OAS), 87, 110, 135, 149, 172
Orinoco River, 8
Orozco, José Clemente, 70, 91

padrino, 72
Palma, Tomás Estrada, 105
Pampas, 10-11; climate, 19
Panama, 1, 2, 18, 126, 127, 133, 168; minerals, 26
Panama Canal, 5, 127, 168
Pan-American conferences, 169
Pan American Health Organization, 149
Pan American Highway, 7, 10
Pan-American Union, 172
Paraguay, 11; minerals, 26
Paraguay River, 12
Paraná Rivér, 8, 11, 12
Patagonian plateau, 10; agriculture, 22-23; climate, 20
patron saints, 66, 88
Pedro (prince), 50, 142, 143
Pedro II, Dom, 142-143
Pelé, 75
peninsulares, 46, 47, 49
Pernambuco, Brazil, 140
personalism, 60
Peru, 2, 5, 7, 8, 67, 156; foods, 74; independence, 51; minerals, 26
Philippines, 84
Picado, Teodoro, 130
piñata, 88
Pinochet, Augusto, 162
pirates, 116
Pizarro, Francisco, 39, 41, 155
plantations, 20, 101, 115, 130
Platt Amendment, 105, 168, 169
political change, 181-182

Pombal, Marquis de, 141
Ponce, Puerto Rico, 114, 115
Ponce de Leon, Juan, 40, 103, 114
Popocatepetl (volcano), 80
population: Brazil, 139, 145, 147; Central America, 126; Chile, 154; Costa Rica, 130; Cuba, 101; growth rate, 179, 181, 182; Mexico, 88; Nicaragua, 132; Puerto Rico, 120
Portales, Diego, 156
Portillo, José Lopez, 86, 97
Porto Alegre, Brazil, 11
Portugal, and the New World, 40, 58, 140, 145; colonial power, 44-48
Posada, José Guadalupe, 91
poverty, 183
Protestantism, 65
publishing, in Latin America, 69
Puebla, Mexico, 80, 96
Puerto Rico, 2, 100, 113-122, 168; agriculture, 115, 121; cities, 114, 115; commonwealth status, 113, 118-119; economy, 117, 121, 122; entertainment, 120; education, 116, 122, emigration to U.S., 121; foods, 114; government, 117-118, 121, 122; history, 117-118, 121, 122; housing, 122; industry, 114, 122; land reform, 121; language, 120; location, 113-114; *map*, 113, "Operation Bootstrap", 117, 121-122; population, 120; religion, 120, topography, 113-114; tourism, 144, 122; the U.S. and, 113, 116-118, 122
pyramids, Mayan, 80

rainfall, *see* climate
Rebélo, Marques, 69
Recife, Brazil, 3, 11, 150
regional trade associations, 173
Rego, José Lins do, 69
Reidy Alfonsó Eduardo, 71

reinols, 50
relationships, business and personal, 60-61
religion, 1, 58, 64-66, 84, 88, 120, 146; Aztecs, 36; Mayas, 32
revolution, Cuban, 106-112
revolution, Nicaraguan, 135-136
Rio de Janeiro, Brazil, 3, 11, 69, 141, 142, 147, 150
Rio Grande, 18, 79, 82, 84
Rivera, Diego, 70, 91
Rodo, José, 68
Roosevelt, Franklin D., 169
Roosevelt, Teddy, 168
Roosevelt Corollary, 168
Rosas, Juan Manuel de, 143
rivers, 7-8, 10, 12

Sá, Mem de, 141
Sacasa, President, 133
Salvador, Brazil, 11, 71, 150
Sandinistas, 135, 136
Sandino, Augusto Cesar, 133, 135
San José, Costa Rica, 129
San Juan, Puerto Rico, 114, 115
San Martín, José de, 48, 49, 155
Santa Anna, Antonio Lopez de, 82-83
Santiago, Chile, 3, 7, 155
Santiago, Cuba, 100
Santos, Brazil, 11
São Lourenco River, 12
São Paulo, Brazil, 11, 147, 150
São Salvador, Brazil, 141
São Vincente, Brazil, 140
Sarmiento, Domingo, 68
sculpture: Mayan, 31
serapes, 89
Sierra Madres, 5, 80
siesta, 88
Siqueiros, David Alfaro, 70, 91
sisal, 93
slaves and slavery, 46, 47, 55, 59, 101, 115, 143, 146

"Soccer War" (1969), 173
social change, 146, 182-184
social security: Mexico, 84, 91
Somoza, Luis, 135
Somoza Debayle, Anastasio, 135, 136, 171
Somoza Garcia, Anastasio, 132, 133, 135
Soto, Hernando de, 104
South America, 139-163; agriculture, 22-23; climate, 18-20; location, 1, 2
Souza, Tomé de, 140
Spain and the New World, 36, 37, 38, 40, 41, 58; colonial power 44-48; in Costa Rica, 129; in Cuba, 103; in Mexico, 81; in Nicaragua, 132; in Puerto Rico, 115
Spanish-American War, 50, 104, 116
sports, 75; Mayan, 32
sugarcane, 20-21, 93, 101-102, 104, 115, 121, 127, 141, 151, 152
Surinam: minerals, 26

Tamayo, Rufino, 91
Tampico, Mexico, 80
Tenochtitlán, 35, 36, 81
Texas, 82
Third World, Latin America as part of, 86, 100, 176, 184
Tierra del Fuego, 5, 10
Tinoco, Federico, 130
Tiradentes (Joaquim José de Silva Xavier), 141
tithe, 64
Titicaca, Lake, 8, 139
tobacco, 21, 101, 102, 121, 152
Toltecs, 80
topography, 3-10; in Brazil, 139-140; in Chile, 154; in Costa Rica, 129; in Cuba, 100-101; in Mexico, 79-80; in Nicaragua, 131, in Puerto Rico, 113-114
Tordesillas, Treaty of, 140
tourism, 114, 122, 151

trade, 54, 174-175; Brazil, 142, 152, 154; Chile, 159; during colonial period, 45; Mexico, 93, 94, 95
transportation, 7, 10, 27, 84, 129, 142
Trinidad, 2
Tropic of Cancer, 5, 14
Tropic of Capricorn, 5, 14
Truman, Harry, 119

Union of Soviet Socialist Republics (U.S.S.R.): Chile and, 162, 163; Cuba and, 109-110
United Nations, 119
United States, 166-172; aid, 169; Brazil and, 151; Chile and, 156, 161, 162; Cuba and, 104-105, 107, 109, 110, 111; inter-American relations, 167-172; 172; Mexico and, 55, 82-84, 86; Nicaragua and, 133, 135, 136; Puerto Rico and, 113, 116-118; Spanish American War, 68
University of Mexico, 88
urbanization, 179, 182
Uruguay, 2, 8; foods, 74
Uruguay River, 8
Uspallata Pass, 7

Valdivia, Pedro de, 155
Vasconcelos, 59
Vasquez de Coronado, Juan, 129
Vega, Garcilaso de la, 67
vegetation, 12, 13
Velásquez, Diego, 103
Venezuela, 2, 8, 13, 139, 167, 173; foods, 74; mineral resources, 27
Vera Cruz, Mexico, 80, 93, 96
Vilella, Roberto Sanchez, 119
Villa, Pancho, 83
Virgin Islands, 2
volcanos, 127

Walker, William, 133
War of the Pacific (1879), 156, 158, 173

War of the Triple Alliance (1865) 172

water supply projects, 149

weather, *see* climate

West Indies, 2, 99, 130; agriculture, 20-24; climate, 15-17

Wood, General Leonard, 104

World War II, 84, 105, 121, 169

yerba maté, 11

Yucatán, 18, 31, 79, 80, 93

zambos, 58

Zapata, Emiliano, 83